Developing Listening Skills 1

 Compass Publishing

Developing Listening Skills 1

Casey Malarcher

Acquisitions Editor: Andrea Janzen
Cover/Interior Design: Design Plus

ISBN: 1-932222-28-6

06 05

[C][O][N][T][E][N][T][S]

First Meeting

A. Look & Listen   Listen to the dialogs.

B. Match   Listen again. Match the people who meet.

1. Joe   · Sarah
2. Gloria   · Karen
3. Greg's wife   · Larry
4. Ellen   · Steve

C. Practice   Practice these sentences from the dialogs.

1. A: Hi, Joe. I'm Karen Fisher.
   B: Oh! You must be Ellen's sister.

2. A: Larry, it's me! Gloria!
   B: Oh my gosh! Gloria! I didn't recognize you.

3. A: Sarah, let me introduce you to my wife.
   B: Hello. It's so nice to finally meet you.

4. A: Hi. I don't believe we've met. I'm Ellen.
   B: It's a pleasure to meet you, Ellen. My name is Steve.

A. How would you answer? Listen. Write the answer.

| Hi. I'm Paula. | Not at all. Have a seat. | Not much. |
| How do you do? | No, I don't believe we have. | |

1. _____
2. _____
3. _____
4. _____
5. _____

B. How would you ask? Listen. Write the question or statement.

| How is it going? | It's a pleasure to meet you. | What's up? |
| Is this seat taken? | Hi. I'm Lisa. What's your name? | |

1. _____
2. _____
3. _____
4. _____
5. _____

C. Picture Description Describe the picture using the words below.

| sit | stand | talk | book |

_____
_____
_____
_____
_____

Listen to the description of the picture.

A. Vocabulary Listen to the words and repeat them.

1. (A) Mr.   (B) Mrs.   (C) Miss   (D) Ms.

2. (A) fine   (B) not bad   (C) great   (D) pretty good

3. (A) friend   (B) neighbor   (C) colleague   (D) co-worker

4. (A) met   (B) seen   (C) heard   (D) introduced

5. (A) brother   (B) sister   (C) uncle   (D) aunt

Now listen to the dialogs and circle the word you hear.

B. Conversation Pictures Listen to the dialogs and number the pictures.

Now listen to the dialogs again and choose the correct relationship.

1. (A) classmates   (B) co-workers   (C) old friends   (D) relatives

2. (A) classmates   (B) co-workers   (C) old friends   (D) relatives

3. (A) classmates   (B) co-workers   (C) old friends   (D) relatives

4. (A) classmates   (B) co-workers   (C) old friends   (D) relatives

A. Dialog 1 Listen to the dialog and questions. Choose the best answer.

1. (A) at a party   (B) in a classroom
   (C) on a bus   (D) on the street

2. (A) their addresses   (B) their ages
   (C) their names   (D) their friends

Listen again. Fill in the blanks.

W: Excuse me. Is this seat taken?

M: No, it's not. Please (1)_____.

W: Thanks. My name is Julia.

M: Hi, Julia. I'm Rick. Nice (2)_____ you.

W: Nice to meet you, too. Wow! There sure are a lot of
   (3)_____ in this class.

M: Yeah. This class is required for all freshmen.

B. Dialog 2 Listen to the dialog and questions. Choose the best answer.

1. (A) to ask her questions   (B) to find out her name
   (C) to make friends   (D) to welcome her

2. (A) ask him questions   (B) leave the office
   (C) not talk to him   (D) talk to him

Listen again. Fill in the blanks.

M: Hello, Dr. Collins? May I (1)_____?

W: Yes, of course. Please have a seat.

M: My name is Dan Goodwin. I'm with the Denver Times.

W: How may I help you, Mr. Goodwin?

M: I'm (2)_____ an article on college freshmen, and I'd
   like to ask you some questions.

W: I'll be happy (3)_____. What questions would you like
   to ask me?

A. Listen Choose the best answer.

1. Which is true about the woman and the man?
   (A) They are in the wrong seats. (B) They are traveling together.
   (C) They don't know each other. (D) They work for the same airline.

2. Who talks about his or her job?
   (A) the woman (B) the man
   (C) both of them (D) neither of them

3. What do we learn about the man?
   (A) his age (B) his hometown
   (C) his name (D) his sister's job

B. Listen again Fill in the blanks.

W: Excuse me. That's my seat by the window.

M: Oh. Sorry. Let me move my (1)_____.

W: Thanks. This flight sure is full today.

M: This is the peak travel season. Are you going to Berlin for business or pleasure?

W: Business. I'm (2)_____ a conference there.

M: Really? What kind of conference is it?

W: It is a (3)_____ conference. What about you? What will you be doing in Berlin?

M: I'm going to visit my (4)_____. This is actually my first time to visit Germany.

W: Me, too. I've been to Europe several times before, but this will be my first visit to Germany.

M: (5)_____, my name is Phillip.

W: Nice to meet you, Phillip. I'm Wendy.

M: You know, I've never met a mathematician before . . .

A. Listen & Choose Choose the best answer.

1. What is the main idea?
   (A) They work together. (B) They have the same interest.
   (C) They like parties. (D) They fell in love.

2. Where did they meet?
   (A) at a conference (B) at a party
   (C) in a store (D) on an airplane

Listen again. Fill in the blanks.

I met this really interesting woman named Olivia
(1)_____ last weekend. She said she works for a web
design company. But as we were talking, I found out she
(2)_____ work as a professional photographer. I like
(3)_____, too. Photography is my hobby.

B. Listen & Choose Choose the best answer.

1. What is this advertisement for?
   (A) a book (B) a class
   (C) a club (D) a conference

2. What should people do to sign up?
   (A) call (B) go online
   (C) mail in a form (D) meet on Oct. 3

Listen again. Fill in the blanks.

Are you (1)_____? Do you want to act and speak with
more confidence? Then you should sign up for Dr.
Kramer's Public Speaking (2)_____! The class will
meet once a week for eight weeks starting on October
3rd. Call 1-888-952-6000 and (3)_____ today!

PUBLIC SPEAKING
SIGN UP TODAY!

A. Picture Matching Listen to the dialog. Choose the correct picture.

Ⓐ **Ⓑ** **Ⓒ**

1. (A) (B) (C)

2. (A) (B) (C)

B. Listen & Choose Listen to the dialog and question. Choose the best answer.

1. (A) They don't know each other. (B) They know each other.
    (C) They study together. (D) They work together.

2. (A) in a dormitory (B) in a park
    (C) in a store (D) on an airplane

3. (A) their ages (B) their hometowns
    (C) their jobs (D) their names

4. (A) her friend (B) her neighbor
    (C) her aunt (D) her colleague

5. (A) the food (B) the people
    (C) the weekend (D) the weather

6. (A) Mary (B) Dottie
    (C) Ms. Williams (D) Mrs. Williams

7. (A) in a classroom (B) in a house
    (C) in an office (D) at a bus stop

R e a d i n g

A. Pre-reading Discussion

Talk about these questions.

1. What do you talk about when you meet someone for the first time?

2. What shouldn't you talk about when you meet someone for the first time?

3. What are "taboo" topics you shouldn't talk about when you meet Americans?

Different cultures have different ways to meet and greet people. For example, in many Asian countries, it is polite to bow or nod your head as a greeting. In Western countries, it is polite to shake hands. And between close friends, people in some Latin countries greet each other with a kiss on the cheek. When traveling in another country, just "do as the Romans do" and copy the actions of the people you meet.

After greeting another person and telling her or him your name, you need a good topic to talk about. The best thing is to look around and talk about your situation. Are you at a party? Talk about the party. Are you in school? Talk about school. It is not a good idea to ask very personal questions when you meet someone for the first time. Wait until you know a person fairly well before you bring up personal topics like a person's age, marital status, or political or religious beliefs.

B. Reading Comprehension

Answer the following questions from the reading.

1. How would people probably greet each other in Japan? In Canada? In Spain?

2. What would be a good topic to talk about with someone you meet at a wedding?

3. What topics shouldn't you talk about with Americans unless you know them well?

Listening Test

Part I: Picture Description

Choose the statement that best describes what you see in the picture.

1.

(A)   (B)   (C)   (D)

2.

(A)   (B)   (C)   (D)

3.

(A)   (B)   (C)   (D)

4.

(A)   (B)   (C)   (D)

5.

(A)   (B)   (C)   (D)

Part II: Questions and Responses

Listen to the question and choose the best answer.

1. (A)   (B)   (C)

2. (A)   (B)   (C)

3. (A)   (B)   (C)

4. (A)   (B)   (C)

5. (A)   (B)   (C)

Part III: Short Conversations

Choose the best answer to each question.

1. What does the woman prefer to be called?
   (A) her first name
   (B) her full name
   (C) her last name
   (D) her nickname

2. How does the man respond to the woman?
   (A) He asks her to have coffee.
   (B) He says things are fine.
   (C) He tells her it is a bad day.
   (D) He wants to complain.

3. Which is probably true about the woman?
   (A) She has never met the man.
   (B) She is the man's boss.
   (C) She was late for a meeting.
   (D) She was sick before.

4. What will the man do?
   (A) get Rhonda a drink
   (B) give Rhonda his phone number
   (C) introduce his friend to Rhonda
   (D) see Rhonda later

5. What is true about the man and woman?
   (A) They don't know each other.
   (B) They have a friend named Susan.
   (C) They will be in the same class.
   (D) They work together.

Part IV: Short Talks

Choose the best answer to each question.

1. Who is introducing himself?
   (A) a freshman
   (B) a professor
   (C) a reporter
   (D) a tour guide

2. Which is true about the speaker?
   (A) He designs university buildings.
   (B) He plans to open a university.
   (C) He studies at the university.
   (D) He teaches at the university.

3. Who is the speaker talking to?
   (A) parents and future students
   (B) his roommate
   (C) students graduating from the university
   (D) university faculty

4. Who is the woman introducing?
   (A) a politician
   (B) a prize winner
   (C) an invited speaker
   (D) herself

5. Which is true about Elizabeth Berkley?
   (A) She came from a poor family.
   (B) She has written articles and a book.
   (C) She grew up on Wall Street.
   (D) She won a lot of money.

A. Look & Listen   Listen to the dialogs.

B. Match   Listen again. Match the person with the action.

1. Rosemary   · eating
2. Jason   · playing
3. Charles   · sitting
4. Kate   · standing

C. Practice   Practice these sentences from the dialogs.

1. A: Who is the woman sitting in the chair?
   B: That is my grandmother.

2. A: Do you see them often?
   B: Yes. We usually get together about once a month.

3. A: He looks very similar to your father.
   B: He is my father's older brother.

4. A: Who is the woman feeding the baby?
   B: She is my Aunt Karen.

A. How would you answer? Listen. Write the answer.

No, she doesn't.   Just one.   Yes, I am.
My aunt Janet.   No, it's not that big.

1. _____

2. _____

3. _____

4. _____

5. _____

B. How would you ask? Listen. Write the question or statement.

Does he play golf?   Who are they?   Do they live with you?
How many cousins do you have?   Is she older or younger than you?

1. _____

2. _____

3. _____

4. _____

5. _____

C. Picture Description   Describe the picture using the words below.

hand   park   point   shoulders

_____

_____

_____

_____

_____

_____

Listen to the description of the picture.

A. Vocabulary Listen to the words and repeat them.

1. (A) father   (B) mother   (C) brother   (D) cousin
2. (A) aunt   (B) uncle   (C) sister   (D) niece
3. (A) nephew   (B) grandmother (C) grandfather (D) in-law
4. (A) older   (B) younger   (C) middle   (D) only
5. (A) best friend   (B) neighbor   (C) classmate   (D) family

Now listen to the dialogs and circle the word you hear.

B. Conversation Pictures Listen to the dialogs and number the pictures.

Now listen to the dialogs again and choose the correct relationship.

1. (A) brothers   (B) co-workers   (C) neighbors   (D) sisters
2. (A) brothers   (B) co-workers   (C) neighbors   (D) sisters
3. (A) brothers   (B) co-workers   (C) neighbors   (D) sisters
4. (A) brothers   (B) co-workers   (C) neighbors   (D) sisters

A. Dialog 1 Listen to the dialog and questions. Choose the best answer.

1. (A) his aunt   (B) his friend
    (C) his mother   (D) his sister

2. (A) It's small.   (B) It's big.
    (C) It's average.   (D) It's like hers.

Listen again. Fill in the blanks.

> W: I saw you yesterday in the park. Who was the woman you were with?
> M: That was my (1)_____, Catherine.
> W: I thought you only had an older (2)_____.
> M: Actually, I have an older brother and two (3)_____ sisters.
> W: Wow! You've got a big family.
> M: Yeah. I guess it's bigger than most people's families.

B. Dialog 2 Listen to the dialog and questions. Choose the best answer.

1. (A) her cousin   (B) her friend
    (C) her in-law   (D) her sister

2. (A) She has a boyfriend.   (B) Her brother is the woman's boyfriend.
    (C) The man is her boyfriend.   (D) Her boyfriend is older than her.

Listen again. Fill in the blanks.

> M: Where did your friend go? I wanted to meet her.
> W: She had to leave. She promised to (1)_____ someone at 2 o'clock.
> M: Oh. By the way, what is her name?
> W: Her name is Brenda.
> M: I sure hope you can (2)_____ me to Brenda some day.
> W: I'd be glad to. And I'll also introduce you to her (3)_____.

A. Listen Choose the best answer.

1. Who gave the woman flowers?
  (A) her best friend
  (B) her boyfriend
  (C) her co-worker
  (D) her sister

2. How did the two women meet?
  (A) in church
  (B) at work
  (C) through friends
  (D) in school

3. Which is true about the two women?
  (A) They communicate often.
  (B) They don't communicate.
  (C) The rarely communicate.
  (D) They occasionally communicate.

B. Listen again Fill in the blanks.

M: The flowers on your desk are very nice. Who sent them to you?
W: Patricia, my (1)_____.
M: I think you've told me about her before. Wasn't she your old high school friend?
W: I met her before high school. We actually (2)_____ together.
M: So how long have you known each other?
W: Let me see. I guess we've known each other since elementary school. So we've been friends for almost (3)_____ years!
M: That's a long time.
W: Yeah, in some ways I feel like she's almost my (4)_____.
M: Do you two still (5)_____ with each other?
W: Sure. We write to each other by email several times a week.

A. Listen & Choose Choose the best answer.

1. How did he meet his best friend?
    (A) They had a class together.
    (B) They lived next to each other.
    (C) They volunteered together.
    (D) They were roommates.

2. Which is true?
    (A) His friend is older than him.
    (B) His friend is younger than him.
    (C) They are the same age.
    (D) He does not know his friend's age.

Listen again. Fill in the blanks.

My best friend is Michael. We've known each other since (1)_____. We didn't have any classes together because he is one year (2)_____ than me. I met him when I volunteered to work on the school's newspaper. He was the school newspaper's (3)_____.

B. Listen & Choose Choose the best answer.

1. Who are Matt and Frieda?
    (A) her children
    (B) her friends
    (C) her neighbors
    (D) her relatives

2. Which is true about Matt and Frieda?
    (A) They don't want children.
    (B) They have many children.
    (C) They have no children.
    (D) They travel with children.

Listen again. Fill in the blanks.

I think my Uncle Matt and Aunt Frieda are very interesting. Uncle Matt is my (1)_____ younger brother. He married Aunt Frieda (2)_____ years ago, but they still don't have any children. I think they are interesting because they like to travel to other countries. They have traveled (3)_____ Europe, Asia, and South America.

A. Picture Matching Listen to the dialog. Choose the correct picture.

Ⓐ Ⓑ Ⓒ

1.	(A)	(B)	(C)
2.	(A)	(B)	(C)

B. Listen & Choose Listen to the dialog and question. Choose the best answer.

1. (A) brothers (B) co-workers
   (C) cousins (D) friends

2. (A) her friend (B) her nephew
   (C) her parents (D) her sister

3. (A) how old she is (B) how she looks
   (C) what her job is (D) who her boyfriend is

4. (A) his ex-girlfriend (B) his friend's ex-girlfriend
   (C) his friend's girlfriend (D) his friend's sister

5. (A) his brother's (B) his grandfather's
   (C) his father's (D) his uncle's

6. (A) his friends and co-workers (B) just his grandfather
   (C) many of his relatives (D) only his brothers and sisters

7. (A) He is not alive. (B) He lives in Vancouver.
   (C) He moved. (D) He works far away.

Reading

A. Pre-reading Discussion

Talk about these questions.

1. How many children did your grandparents have?

2. How many children do your parents have?

3. How many children would you like to have?

In the 1950s, most families in the United States included four people, two parents and two children. Since that time, the size of the American family has become smaller. In 1970, the average American family had only three people. And in 2000, the average American family only had 2.5 people. That means for every one hundred married couples, only fifty of the couples had children. And of the couples with children, these parents only had one child.

Of course these numbers are only for the average family. It is true that White, Black, and Asian families now have fewer children than in the past, but the size of Hispanic families has not changed much. However, in general it is rare today to find a family in America with more than three children.

Although the size of the family has gone down in the United States, the average size of the American house has grown. In 1970, the first house a new family bought was usually 140 square meters. In 2000, a new family's first home was more than 200 square meters.

B. Reading Comprehension

Answer the following questions from the reading.

1. How many children did the average family have in the 1950s?

2. How many children does the average family have today?

3. How has the size of first homes changed in the United States?

Listening Test

Part I: Picture Description

Choose the statement that best describes what you see in the picture.

1.

   (A)   (B)   (C)   (D)

2.

   (A)   (B)   (C)   (D)

3.

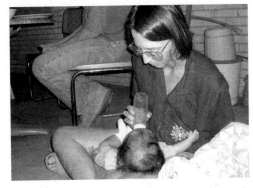

   (A)   (B)   (C)   (D)

4.

(A)   (B)   (C)   (D)

5.

(A)   (B)   (C)   (D)

Part II: Questions and Responses

Listen to the question and choose the best answer.

1. (A)   (B)   (C)

2. (A)   (B)   (C)

3. (A)   (B)   (C)

4. (A)   (B)   (C)

5. (A)   (B)   (C)

Part III: Short Conversations

Choose the best answer to each question.

1. What does the man's reply mean?
   (A) I don't understand.
   (B) Let's do them together later.
   (C) No, thank you.
   (D) Yes, I would like your help.

2. What does the man say is a bad point about the house?
   (A) It has a small yard.
   (B) It is downtown.
   (C) It has many rooms.
   (D) It is too big.

3. What is the woman's opinion of the picture?
   (A) It is very funny.
   (B) It looks professional.
   (C) The man looks older in it.
   (D) The man's brother is handsome.

4. Why doesn't he want to buy jewelry?
   (A) He may make a bad choice.
   (B) His grandmother is old.
   (C) It is too expensive.
   (D) The party is tomorrow.

5. What is shown in the picture?
   (A) a teenage boy
   (B) a teenager girl
   (C) a baby boy
   (D) a baby girl

Part IV: Short Talks

Choose the best answer to each question.

1. What is being advertised?
   - (A) a new store
   - (B) a television program
   - (C) a web site
   - (D) lost relatives

2. What can people get from this service?
   - (A) children
   - (B) free gifts
   - (C) new friends
   - (D) information

3. Who is Kevin?
   - (A) his brother
   - (B) his cousin
   - (C) his friend
   - (D) his nephew

4. Which is true about his relationship with Kevin?
   - (A) They are in love with the same girl.
   - (B) They did not like each other for many years.
   - (C) They do not know each other well.
   - (D) They have know each other many years.

5. Where is this speech being given?
   - (A) at a business meeting
   - (B) at a conference
   - (C) at a picnic
   - (D) at a wedding

Warm-up

A. Look & Listen   Listen to the dialogs.

B. Match   Listen again. Match the activity with the time.

1. collecting
2. reading
3. in-line skating
4. playing guitar

· years ago
· last year
· now
· in the future

C. Practice   Practice these sentences from the dialogs.

1. A: I used to collect them.
   B: You don't collect them anymore?

2. A: What book are you reading?
   B: I finished a book about Cleopatra's life last week.

3. A: Isn't in-line skating hard?
   B: No, it's easy.

4. A: How long have you been playing the guitar?
   B: I started playing it last year.

A. How would you answer? Listen. Write the answer.

> No, I'm not.   Not very well.   Sure, that's fine.
> Yes, I do.   Two or three times a month.

1. _____
2. _____
3. _____
4. _____
5. _____

B. How would you ask? Listen. Write the question or statement.

> Do you enjoy cooking?   How often do you play tennis?
> Can you ice skate?   Do you have any plans for this weekend?
> What do you like to do in your free time?

1. _____
2. _____
3. _____
4. _____
5. _____

C. Picture Description Describe the picture using the words below.

> plant   garden   water   wear

_____

_____

_____

_____

_____

Listen to the description of the picture.

A. Vocabulary Listen to the words and repeat them.

1. (A) weekend (B) holiday (C) vacation (D) break time
2. (A) exciting (B) interesting (C) boring (D) relaxing
3. (A) hiking (B) jogging (C) racing (D) walking
4. (A) listen to (B) play (C) read (D) watch
5. (A) sometimes (B) all the time (C) every day (D) once a week

Now listen to the dialogs and circle the word you hear.

B. Conversation Pictures Listen to the dialogs and number the pictures.

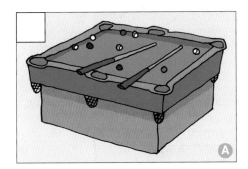

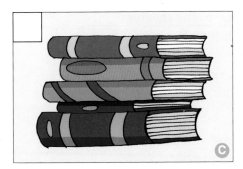

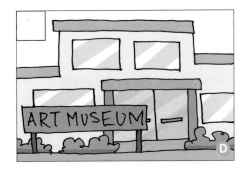

Now listen to the dialogs again and choose the correct time of each activity.

1. (A) past (B) present (C) future
2. (A) past (B) present (C) future
3. (A) past (B) present (C) future
4. (A) past (B) present (C) future

A. Dialog 1 Listen to the dialog and questions. Choose the best answer.

1. (A) a library
   (C) a place for exercising
   (B) a park
   (D) a place with stores

2. (A) playing music
   (C) looking around
   (B) watching videos
   (D) working out

Listen again. Fill in the blanks.

W: What do you like to do in your free time?
M: I like to hang out at (1)_____.
W: Really? I didn't know you liked shopping so much.
M: I don't shop. I spend most of my time playing
   (2)_____ or just window shopping in bookstores or
   (3)_____ stores.

B. Dialog 2 Listen to the dialog and questions. Choose the best answer.

1. (A) a drama
   (C) a horror movie
   (B) a romantic comedy
   (D) an action movie

2. (A) continue reading
   (C) rent a video
   (B) go to the theater
   (D) talk to the man

Listen again. Fill in the blanks.

M: What are you doing?
W: I'm just (1)_____. What are you doing?
M: Nothing. I'm bored. Let's go see a movie.
W: Are there any good movies at the theater?
M: Sure! There is a new James Bond movie that just (2)_____.
W: No, thanks. I think I'll just finish (3)_____.

A. Listen Choose the best answer.

1. What is the man's hobby?
   (A) driving
   (B) reading books
   (C) sailing boats
   (D) working on his car

2. Which is true about the man?
   (A) He has more than one car.
   (B) He is a mechanic.
   (C) His wife does not drive.
   (D) His car is not very good.

3. How does her grandfather feel about boats?
   (A) He ignores them.
   (B) He likes them a lot.
   (C) They make him mad.
   (D) They need a lot of work.

B. Listen again Fill in the blanks.

W: I saw you working on your car this afternoon. Is it broken again?

M: No, I wasn't fixing my car. I was (1)_____ the engine.

W: You seem to take good care of your car. I see you working on it all the time.

M: I guess working on my car is my hobby.

W: How can your car be your hobby?

M: Well, I read books about ways to (2)_____ my car. And I like to buy new parts for my car.

W: When do you have time to drive it?

M: I only drive this car on (3)_____. I like to go for long drives in the country with it. My wife and I use our other car for driving around in the city.

W: Your hobby is (4)_____ my grandfather's hobby.

M: What is your grandfather's hobby?

W: Fixing and taking care of boats. He's (5)_____ about sailboats.

A. Listen & Choose Choose the best answer.

1. When does she have free time?
(A) at night   (B) in the morning
(C) on Friday   (D) on weekends

2. What does she do in her free time?
(A) goes to movies   (B) meets her friends
(C) reads books   (D) watches television

Listen again. Fill in the blanks.

I have a lot of homework every day. But I still can enjoy a
little free time (1)_____. After dinner, I usually watch
television for (2)_____ before I start working on my
homework. These days, I enjoy watching a (3)_____
about three women living together in a house in Los Angeles.

B. Listen & Choose Choose the best answer.

1. Why doesn't he have much free time on Saturdays?
(A) He has to work.   (B) He has two jobs.
(C) His apartment is large. (D) His parents visit him.

2. How much free time does he have each week?
(A) an hour each night   (B) two full days
(C) only one day   (D) none

Listen again. Fill in the blanks.

In my office, we have to work for half a day on Saturday, so I
don't have much free time on the weekend. When I finish
work on Saturday, I (1)_____ have to go to the store to
do some shopping. I also have to do my (2)_____ chores
on Saturday, like cleaning my apartment and doing laundry.
Sunday is my only day for (3)_____ during the week.

A. Picture Matching Listen to the dialog. Choose the correct picture.

Ⓐ　　　　　　　　Ⓑ　　　　　　　　Ⓒ

1.　　　(A)　　　　　　　(B)　　　　　　　(C)

2.　　　(A)　　　　　　　(B)　　　　　　　(C)

B. Listen & Choose Listen to the dialog and question. Choose the best answer.

1. (A) collecting beds　　　　　　(B) collecting boxes
　　 (C) collecting postcards　　　　(D) collecting stamps

2. (A) see animals　　　　　　　(B) travel
　　 (C) visit his parents　　　　　(D) watch a movie

3. (A) plays a sport　　　　　　(B) studies
　　 (C) tutors other students　　　(D) works at a store

4. (A) He does not like TV.　　　(B) He rarely watches TV.
　　 (C) He should buy a TV.　　　(D) He watches TV a lot.

5. (A) movies and sports　　　　(B) music shows and news
　　 (C) news and movies　　　　　(D) sports and music shows

6. (A) Chinese　　　　　　　　(B) French
　　 (C) Italian　　　　　　　　(D) Middle Eastern

7. (A) help him　　　　　　　(B) leave
　　 (C) not help him　　　　　　(D) order some food

R e a d i n g

A. Pre-reading Discussion

Talk about these questions.

1. How much free time do you have each day? On weekends?

2. In general, who has more free time, men or women?

3. What do you do in your free time?

Researchers in Australia wanted to find out how people spent their free time. The researchers asked people to write down all of the activities they did for two days.

Through the survey, most Australians said they had between four and five hours of free time each day during the week. On weekends they had between six and seven hours of free time. In comparing the free time available to men and women, the researchers found that men had a little more free time than women. This was probably because women spend more time doing housework and taking care of children.

During the two-day research period, 88% of the people taking the survey said they spent time watching TV or videos. 75% said they enjoyed time socializing with family or friends. 57% said they spent time listening to music, and 48% spent time reading. Only 27% said they played sports or exercised, and less than 6% watched a sporting event. It was also found that people often did more than one free time activity at the same time. For example, many people reported socializing as their free time activity, but they also mentioned watching TV at the same time.

B. Reading Comprehension

Answer the following questions from the reading.

1. How long did the researchers do this study?

2. Who has more free time, Australian men or women?

3. What is the most popular free time activity for Australians?

Listening Test

Part I: Picture Description

Choose the statement that best describes what you see in the picture.

1.

    (A)   (B)   (C)   (D)

2.

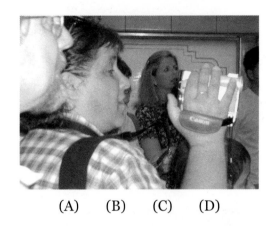

    (A)   (B)   (C)   (D)

3.

    (A)   (B)   (C)   (D)

4.

(A)   (B)   (C)   (D)

5.

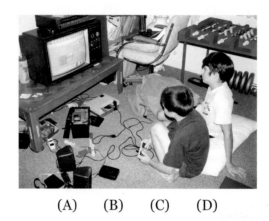

(A)   (B)   (C)   (D)

Part II: Questions and Responses

Listen to the question and choose the best answer.

1. (A)   (B)   (C)

2. (A)   (B)   (C)

3. (A)   (B)   (C)

4. (A)   (B)   (C)

5. (A)   (B)   (C)

Part III: Short Conversations

Choose the best answer to each question.

1. What does the woman's last statement mean?
   (A) I can't remember.
   (B) I changed my mind.
   (C) It does not work.
   (D) It is no trouble for me.

2. Where will they sit?
   (A) above the stage
   (B) behind the stage
   (C) near the stage
   (D) on the stage

3. What kind of movie did the man probably see?
   (A) a comedy
   (B) a documentary
   (C) a horror movie
   (D) animation

4. Which is true of the opinions of the woman and the man?
   (A) They agree.
   (B) They don't agree.
   (C) They have no opinion.
   (D) They are joking.

5. Where is this conversation probably taking place?
   (A) at a breakfast table
   (B) in a dark movie theater
   (C) in an office at lunch time
   (D) outside at night

Part IV: Short Talks

Choose the best answer to each question.

1. What should students make for the contest?
   (A) a science project
   (B) a special shirt
   (C) a speech
   (D) a piece of work

2. What will the winner receive?
   (A) a painting
   (B) a trip to Paris
   (C) money
   (D) nothing

3. When will the winner be announced?
   (A) November 1st
   (B) later today
   (C) in November
   (D) next week

4. What should be drawn first?
   (A) an "O"
   (B) an "X"
   (C) a row of squares
   (D) a player

5. Which player puts a mark first?
   (A) the O player
   (B) the X player
   (C) the older player
   (D) the winner

Date and Time

A. Look & Listen Listen to the dialogs.

B. Match Listen again. Match the day and the plan.

1. Friday   · go shopping
2. Wednesday   · meet club members
3. weekend   · have a holiday
4. Thursday   · go to a party

C. Practice Practice these sentences from the dialogs.

1. A: When is our next essay due?
   B: It's due in two weeks.

2. A: Does the meeting start at 3:45?
   B: No, we're going to start at 4.

3. A: Which day is it?
   B: It's next weekend.

4. A: Are you free later in the week?
   B: Yes, I'm free on Thursday.

A. How would you answer? Listen. Write the answer.

> At 7:30.   How about 5:30?   No, we're not.
> From the 15th.   Tuesday.

1. _____

2. _____

3. _____

4. _____

5. _____

B. How would you ask? Listen. Write the question or statement.

> What time will it arrive?   When will the package be delivered?
> When do you want to meet?   Which day is best for you?
> Which day is the concert on?

1. _____

2. _____

3. _____

4. _____

5. _____

C. Picture Description Describe the picture using the words below.

> calendar   clock   pencil   write

_____

_____

_____

_____

_____

_____

Listen to the description of the picture.

A. Vocabulary Listen to the words and repeat them.

1. (A) Monday   (B) Tuesday   (C) Wednesday   (D) Thursday
2. (A) morning   (B) afternoon   (C) evening   (D) night
3. (A) arrange   (B) get together   (C) meet   (D) schedule
4. (A) after breakfast   (B) around noon   (C) before dinner   (D) at midnight
5. (A) minute   (B) moment   (C) second   (D) soon

Now listen to the dialogs and circle the word you hear.

B. Conversation Pictures Listen to the dialogs and number the pictures.

Now listen to the dialogs again and choose the correct day.

1. (A) Monday   (B) Wednesday   (C) Thursday   (D) Saturday
2. (A) Monday   (B) Wednesday   (C) Thursday   (D) Saturday
3. (A) Monday   (B) Wednesday   (C) Thursday   (D) Saturday
4. (A) Monday   (B) Wednesday   (C) Thursday   (D) Saturday

A. Dialog 1 Listen to the dialog and questions. Choose the best answer.

1. (A) the man's   (B) the woman's
   (C) the man's brother's   (D) the woman's sister's

2. (A) a week day   (B) a week night
   (C) a weekend afternoon   (D) a Sunday evening

Listen again. Fill in the blanks.

W: When is your brother's birthday party?
M: It's on the nineteenth.
W: Great! The nineteenth is a (1)_____ this month.
M: Right. So the party is going to start early in the (2)_____.
W: What time will the party start?
M: My brother told everyone to come around (3)_____ o'clock.

B. Dialog 2 Listen to the dialog and questions. Choose the best answer.

1. (A) She has a class.   (B) She is going shopping.
   (C) She is working.   (D) She does not say.

2. (A) at her house   (B) at his house
   (C) at the bus stop   (D) at the theater

Listen again. Fill in the blanks.

M: Would you like to go to the mall this weekend?
W: Sure. When?
M: (1)_____ is fine.
W: I'm (2)_____ on Saturday. How about Sunday?
M: Sunday is good for me. Do you want to meet in the afternoon?
W: OK. Let's meet at (3)_____ at 3 on Sunday afternoon.

A. Listen Choose the best answer.

1. What will they do when they meet?
   (A) have dinner
   (C) see a movie
   (B) look for a book
   (D) study

2. Why can't she meet on Wednesday?
   (A) She has a class.
   (C) She works in the library.
   (B) She plays a sport.
   (D) She has to cook dinner.

3. When will they meet?
   (A) in the morning
   (C) late in the afternoon
   (B) early in the afternoon
   (D) at night

B. Listen again Fill in the blanks.

M: Do you want to study for the test together?

W: Sure. I'd love to.

M: Great! Can we get together (1)_____ this week?

W: I have a soccer game on Wednesday night.
   How about (2)_____?

M: OK. That day works for me. What time?

W: We should meet a bit early. The test is over three chapters from
   the book.

M: Yeah, and I didn't understand the last
   chapter very well. I want to ask you a
   lot of questions about that one.

W: Why don't we meet at
   (3)_____ in the library? We
   can stay there until it closes at 10.

M: What about dinner?

W: We can just bring some snacks to
   eat while we study.

M: Alright. Then I'll see you
   (4)_____ at
   (5)_____ in the library.

W: Great. See you then.

A. Listen & Choose Choose the best answer.

1. What does Nelson think happened?
   (A) He is in the wrong place.
   (B) He remembered the wrong time.
   (C) Jeff did not get his call.
   (D) Jeff forgot the date.

2. What will he do?
   (A) buy a ticket
   (B) call Jeff's cell phone
   (C) leave
   (D) stay a short time more

Listen again. Fill in the blanks.

Hi, Jeff. This is Nelson. I was just calling to see if you were there. I'm here at the stadium near the north ticket windows. I thought we were supposed to meet here at 1:30, but maybe I had the wrong (1)_____ in mind. If you get this message, (2)_____ on my cell phone. Otherwise, I guess I'll (3)_____ to see if you show up. Bye.

B. Listen & Choose Choose the best answer.

1. Where is the announcement being made?
   (A) at a train station
   (B) in an airport
   (C) on a tour bus
   (D) on an airplane

2. What is probably the problem?
   (A) a bad storm
   (B) no fuel
   (C) engine problems
   (D) bad food

Listen again. Fill in the blanks.

Ladies and gentlemen, we are sorry, but (1)_____ service from Stanton to Deerford has been delayed due to (2)_____ in Deerford. We will make another announcement in half an hour to update you about (3)_____ conditions in Deerford. If conditions have improved, we will begin boarding the flight at that time.

A. Picture Matching Listen to the dialog. Choose the correct picture.

 **A**

 **B**

 **C**

1.   (A)   (B)   (C)

2.   (A)   (B)   (C)

B. Listen & Choose Listen to the dialog and question. Choose the best answer.

1. (A) He works late.   (B) He does not like tennis.
    (C) He will be tired.   (D) He has a late dinner.

2. (A) about ten minutes   (B) less than an hour and a half
    (C) more than two hours   (D) all day

3. (A) She will eat dinner.   (B) The meeting will be short.
    (C) They will be tired.   (D) The streets will be busy.

4. (A) buy his ticket   (B) have coffee
    (C) meet Steve   (D) pick her up

5. (A) at his office   (B) at a coffee shop downtown
    (C) at home   (D) at the airport

6. (A) at noon   (B) in the afternoon
    (C) in the evening   (D) at midnight

7. (A) He is busy.   (B) His friend will come.
    (C) The bakery is large.   (D) The movie is popular.

Reading

A. Pre-reading Discussion

Talk about these questions.

1. Do you like to make plans to use your time wisely?

2. Are you the kind of person who is usually on time or late for appointments?

3. Do you know anyone who is the opposite way? Who?

Did you know some cultures think about time differently than other cultures? They don't read clocks differently. They just understand the importance of time in different ways.

Western cultures like England and the United States have a monochronic view of time. The prefix "mono" means "one", so these cultures think there is only one time, and everyone must follow that time. For these cultures, it is very important to do things at the proper time. They hate being late for appointments. They also think time can be lost or wasted, so it must be used well.

Other cultures, for example some cultures in South America, have a ploychronic view of time. The prefix "poly" means "many", so these cultures think things happen according to their own times. For these cultures, time is flexible and other things may be more important than keeping a strict schedule. In a meeting, people from these cultures may want to take time for socializing. They think it is important to build a relationship with others before starting business.

B. Reading Comprehension

Answer the following questions from the reading.

1. What are the two prefixes defined in the reading? What do they mean?

2. Which view of time probably does not follow exact schedules?

3. Where would things like daily planners sell better, North America or South America?

Listening Test

Part I: Picture Description

Choose the statement that best describes what you see in the picture.

1.

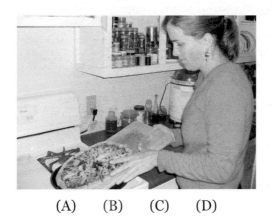

(A)   (B)   (C)   (D)

2.

(A)   (B)   (C)   (D)

3.

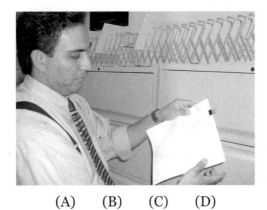

(A)   (B)   (C)   (D)

4.

(A)   (B)   (C)   (D)

5.

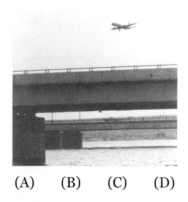

(A)   (B)   (C)   (D)

Part II: Questions and Responses

Listen to the question and choose the best answer.

1. (A)   (B)   (C)

2. (A)   (B)   (C)

3. (A)   (B)   (C)

4. (A)   (B)   (C)

5. (A)   (B)   (C)

Part III: Short Conversations

Choose the best answer to each question.

1. Where does this conversation take place?
   (A) in a taxi
   (B) in an airplane
   (C) on a boat
   (D) on a bus

2. What does the man's statement mean?
   (A) I agree.
   (B) I am bored.
   (C) I didn't hear you.
   (D) I'm not sure.

3. What are these people talking about doing?
   (A) homework
   (B) housework
   (C) paper work
   (D) teamwork

4. What will the woman do?
   (A) buy some medicine
   (B) make an appointment
   (C) meet the man
   (D) see a doctor

5. When is the man not busy?
   (A) all week
   (B) Monday
   (C) Tuesday
   (D) Wednesday

Part IV: Short Talks

Choose the best answer to each question.

1. What does this announcement explain?
   (A) a guest speaker at the conference
   (B) how to sign up for the conference
   (C) the new conference schedule
   (D) where the conference will be held

2. How many people will speak at 2 o'clock?
   (A) none
   (B) one
   (C) two
   (D) three

3. Which has changed for the networking seminar?
   (A) the location
   (B) the speaker
   (C) the time
   (D) the title

4. What is described?
   (A) a bus schedule
   (B) a school's schedule
   (C) a special trip
   (D) an unusual morning

5. Which didn't he do?
   (A) do his homework
   (B) take a quiz
   (C) miss the bus
   (D) sleep late

Telephone

A. Look & Listen   Listen to the dialogs.

B. Match   Listen again. Match the person with the message.

1. mother   · will call Tom again
2. co-worker   · Tom should call
3. sales person   · will see Tom later
4. stranger   · no message

C. Practice   Practice these sentences from the messages.

1. I'll give you another call later tonight.

2. I'll see you around 7:30. Talk to you later.

3. Good afternoon. I'm calling from Good Rates Travel Service.

4. I'm sorry. I think I've got the wrong number.

A. How would you answer? Listen. Write the answer.

> Hello.   Yes, I would. Please tell her Jane called.   No. No message.
> This is his friend, Ray.   Yes, please. Have her call me at home.

1. _____
2. _____
3. _____
4. _____
5. _____

B. How would you ask? Listen. Write the question or statement.

> Can I take a message?   May I have your phone number?
> Who is this?   May I help you?   Can you hear me?

1. _____
2. _____
3. _____
4. _____
5. _____

C. Picture Description Describe the picture using the words below.

> hold   desk   look at   papers

_____

_____

_____

_____

_____

Listen to the description of the picture.

A. Vocabulary Listen to the words and repeat them.

1. (A) give (B) take (C) leave (D) write down
2. (A) can (B) could (C) may (D) would
3. (A) cell phone (B) home (C) number (D) office
4. (A) busy (B) no answer (C) pick up (D) ring
5. (A) collect (B) international (C) local (D) long distance

Now listen to the dialogs and circle the word you hear.

B. Conversation Pictures Listen to the messages and number the pictures.

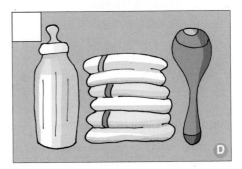

Now listen to the messages again and choose the correct message.

1. (A) Call me. (B) I'll call again. (C) I'll meet you later.
2. (A) Call me. (B) I'll call again. (C) I'll meet you later.
3. (A) Call me. (B) I'll call again. (C) I'll meet you later.
4. (A) Call me. (B) I'll call again. (C) I'll meet you later.

A. Dialog 1 Listen to the dialog and questions. Choose the best answer.

1. (A) to the park   (B) to school
    (C) to work   (D) She does not say.

2. (A) He can't meet Joe.   (B) He will call again.
    (C) Joe will be late.   (D) Joe should call him.

Listen again. Fill in the blanks.

W: Hello?

M: Hi. Is Joe there?

W: No, he's not here at the moment. (1)_____ I take a message?

M: Yes, please. (2)_____ you tell him to call Steve when he gets home?

W: Sure. I'll (3)_____ the message.

M: Thanks. Bye.

B. Dialog 2 Listen to the dialog and questions. Choose the best answer.

1. (A) to call a friend   (B) to eat
    (C) to meet someone   (D) to take pictures

2. (A) very soon   (B) in about twenty minutes
    (C) in an hour   (D) He doesn't know.

Listen again. Fill in the blanks.

M: Good afternoon. Quick Shop Photos. May I help you?

W: Is Mary (1)_____ today?

M: Yes, she is. But she went (2)_____.

W: Do you know when she'll be back?

M: I think she'll be back in about (3)_____ minutes.

W: OK. I'll call back a little later.

A. Listen Choose the best answer.

1. What is Bill probably doing?
   (A) buying something
   (B) exercising
   (C) fixing his car
   (D) studying

2. What kind of club does Bill belong to?
   (A) a drama club
   (B) an English club
   (C) a music club
   (D) a sports club

3. Which is true about the club?
   (A) A new member will join.
   (B) A meeting date has changed.
   (C) It will have a party soon.
   (D) Bill is now president of it.

B. Listen again Fill in the blanks.

W: Hello?

M: Hello. Is Bill there?

W: Bill went to the (1)_____, but he'll be back soon. Can you call back in about twenty minutes?

M: Could you just give him a message for me, instead?

W: Sure. What's the message?

M: The (2)_____ club is not going to meet this week. So our next meeting is going to be on (3)_____ the 24th.

W: No meeting this week. Next meeting is the 24th. (4)_____?

M: That's all.

W: OK, I'll make sure he gets the message when he (5)_____.

M: Thanks. Bye.

W: Bye.

A. Listen & Choose   Choose the best answer.

1. What kind of business is this message for?
    (A) a movie theater   (B) a restaurant
    (C) a sports center   (D) a video game store

2. What should you do to hear directions to this place?
    (A) push number one   (B) push number two
    (C) push number three   (D) hold the line

Listen again. Fill in the blanks.

Thank you for calling Multiplex Entertainment Center. For information on today's shows and (1)_____, press one. For ticket prices and the (2)_____ of this theater, press two. For all other questions, press 3 and your call will be transferred to a (3)_____ manager. To hear these selections again, please stay on the line.

B. Listen & Choose   Choose the best answer.

1. Where was the caller probably trying to call?
    (A) a home   (B) an office
    (C) a school   (D) a store

2. What was for sale?
    (A) furniture   (B) sports equipment
    (C) clothes   (D) baby animals

Listen again. Fill in the blanks.

You have reached the Patterson's (1)_____. No one is available right now to take your call. Please (2)_____ your name and a brief message after the beep. If you are calling for information on the (3)_____ for sale, we are sorry to say they have all been sold. Thanks for calling.

A. Picture Matching   Listen to the dialog. Choose the correct picture.

1.   (A)   (B)   (C)
2.   (A)   (B)   (C)

B. Listen & Choose   Listen to the dialog and question. Choose the best answer.

1. (A) Mary is busy.   (B) Mary answered the phone.
   (C) Mary is out.   (D) The man does not know Mary.

2. (A) a house   (B) a school
   (C) a store   (D) a wrong number

3. (A) Call Shelly ASAP.   (B) Your friend Shelly called.
   (C) Meet Shelly at school.   (D) Shelly is at school.

4. (A) Harry called him.   (B) Harry didn't meet him.
   (C) Joe is bored.   (D) Joe is late.

5. (A) Joe called.   (B) Joe is sorry.
   (C) Joe needs help.   (D) Joe won't be there.

6. (A) A man called.   (B) A saleswoman will call later.
   (C) A woman called.   (D) William got a message.

7. (A) Meet William.   (B) Look for a phone number.
   (C) Call William.   (D) Wait for the man to call.

Reading

A. Pre-reading Discussion

Talk about these questions.

1. What do you say when you answer the phone in your country? What does this mean in English?

2. Do you mind if people call you late at night or early in the morning?

3. What kind of phone technology is popular in your country these days?

Here are some polite rules to follow when calling someone in Canada. If you are the caller, say "hello" and give your name when the person answers the phone.

Another good rule to keep in mind is that you should not call too early or too late. People in Canada respect each other's privacy and this includes their home life. If you call someone before 10 in the morning or after 10 at night, it could bother them or wake them up. Also, remember Canada is a big country. There are several different time zones across the country, so check carefully the time you are calling to make sure it is not too early or too late for the person you are calling.

Many people in Canada have answering machines to take phone messages for them. It is polite to leave a short message, even if it is just your name and that you will call again later. If you think there is a good chance, you will have to leave a message on a machine, you can write your message before you call. This will help you leave a clearer message.

B. Reading Comprehension

Answer the following questions from the reading.

1. After what time in the evening should you not call someone in Canada?

2. Why should you consider the Canadian time zones when you call someone?

3. What suggestion does the reading give if you have to leave a message on a machine?

Listening Test

Part I: Picture Description

Choose the statement that best describes what you see in the picture.

1.

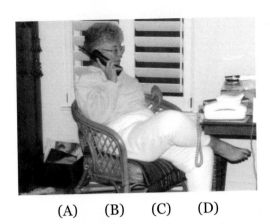

(A)   (B)   (C)   (D)

2.

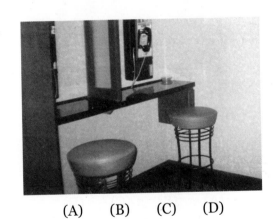

(A)   (B)   (C)   (D)

3.

(A)   (B)   (C)   (D)

4.

(A)   (B)   (C)   (D)

5.

(A)   (B)   (C)   (D)

Part II: Questions and Responses

Listen to the question and choose the best answer.

1. (A)   (B)   (C)

2. (A)   (B)   (C)

3. (A)   (B)   (C)

4. (A)   (B)   (C)

5. (A)   (B)   (C)

Part III: Short Conversations

Choose the best answer to each question.

1. Why will they call the restaurant?
   (A) to check its hours of operation
   (B) to find its location
   (C) to make a reservation
   (D) to order some food

2. What does the man think?
   (A) John is rude.
   (B) John likes the woman.
   (C) John will join them.
   (D) John won't come.

3. Which is true about the message the woman got?
   (A) It is from her friend.
   (B) It is important.
   (C) It is not complete.
   (D) It is old.

4. What will the man do?
   (A) call the woman at home
   (B) give the woman a number
   (C) meet the woman later
   (D) try calling another number

5. Which is true about the woman?
   (A) She called many times.
   (B) She did not know the number.
   (C) She was working late.
   (D) She was worried about the man.

Part IV: Short Talks

Choose the best answer to each question.

1. Where was the caller probably trying to reach?
   (A) a cinema
   (B) a music store
   (C) a theater
   (D) a video store

2. What information is NOT provided in the message?
   (A) location
   (B) prices
   (C) times of operation
   (D) title of show

3. What action does the message suggest the caller take?
   (A) call back another time
   (B) hold the line
   (C) look for a newspaper ad
   (D) press a button

4. Which might be an extension at this office?
   (A) 4
   (B) 42
   (C) 424
   (D) 4242

5. What is implied about speaking to a customer service representative?
   (A) Representatives do not work at night.
   (B) The company has only one.
   (C) The representative is taking a break.
   (D) There may be a wait.

A. Look & Listen   Listen to the dialogs.

B. Match   Listen again. Match the place with the location.

1. subway
2. pharmacy
3. law office
4. bank

· across the street
· around the corner
· two blocks away
· upstairs

C. Practice   Practice these sentences from the dialogs.

1. A: How far away is it?
   B: It's just around the corner.

2. A: There's one across the street.
   B: Really? I don't see it.

3. A: I was told there's a law office in this building.
   B: I think it is up on the fifth floor.

4. A: Where can I find an ATM machine?
   B: There's a bank two blocks down the street.

A. How would you answer? Listen. Write the answer.

Yes, it is.　　I think there is one by the bank.　　Yes, I am.
No, I don't.　　It's that street where the traffic light is.

1. _____

2. _____

3. _____

4. _____

5. _____

B. How would you ask? Listen. Write the question or statement.

Can I buy a map anywhere around here?
Where can I find men's shoes?　　Do you know where City Hall is?
Should I turn here?　　Where is the elevator?

1. _____

2. _____

3. _____

4. _____

5. _____

C. Picture Description Describe the picture using the words below.

backpack　　　　map　　　　point　　　　peak

_____

_____

_____

_____

_____

_____

Listen to the description of the picture.

A. Vocabulary Listen to the words and repeat them.

1. (A) building   (B) corner   (C) floor   (D) street
2. (A) drive   (B) go straight   (C) turn   (D) walk
3. (A) across   (B) down   (C) toward   (D) up
4. (A) miles   (B) houses   (C) blocks   (D) kilometers
5. (A) anywhere   (B) nowhere   (C) where   (D) somewhere

Now listen to the dialogs and circle the word you hear.

B. Conversation Pictures Listen to the dialogs and number the pictures.

Now listen to the dialogs again and choose where the person is going.

1. (A) a classroom   (B) a gate   (C) a town   (D) a university
2. (A) a classroom   (B) a gate   (C) a town   (D) a university
3. (A) a classroom   (B) a gate   (C) a town   (D) a university
4. (A) a classroom   (B) a gate   (C) a town   (D) a university

A. Dialog 1 Listen to the dialog and questions. Choose the best answer.

1. (A) the bathroom   (B) the elevator
   (C) the escalator   (D) the toy department

2. (A) in another store   (B) on another floor
   (C) on the same floor   (D) outside the building

Listen again. Fill in the blanks.

W: Excuse me. Is there (1)_____ on this floor?
M: Yes, ma'am. It's (2)_____ the elevators.
W: Where are the elevators?
M: Walk straight ahead through the (3)_____ and turn left
    at the toy department.
W: Oh yes, I can see the toy department. Thank you.
M: You're welcome.

B. Dialog 2 Listen to the dialog and questions. Choose the best answer.

1. (A) buy a newspaper   (B) eat dinner
   (C) get some money   (D) mail a letter

2. (A) It is not open.   (B) It is on Jefferson.
   (C) It is on the corner.   (D) It is very far away.

Listen again. Fill in the blanks.

M: Is there a (1)_____ near here?
W: Yes, there is one (2)_____ the street from First City Bank.
M: Is that the bank on the corner?
W: No, First City Bank is between the Chinese restaurant and
    bookstore.
M: You mean the bookstore on Jefferson Street?
W: Right. That's the one. The (3)_____ is across the street
    from that.

A. Listen Choose the best answer.

1. Where are they?
   (A) in an airport
   (B) in a hotel
   (C) in a museum
   (D) in a store

2. Where will the bus take the woman?
   (A) to a hotel
   (B) to a museum
   (C) to a shopping mall
   (D) to a subway station

3. How will she know the correct building?
   (A) The gate is pink.
   (B) The driver will tell her.
   (C) The roof is round.
   (D) The walls are green.

B. Listen again Fill in the blanks.

M: Good afternoon. May I help you?
W: Yes, I'd like to visit the art museum. Is it far from this hotel?
M: It's too far to walk. You could (1)_____, but you can also get there easily by bus.
W: I don't mind taking the bus.
M: When you walk out of the hotel, cross the street and you will see a bus stop down the street to your right. You want to take Bus 64 from that stop.
W: Bus 64. Does that bus stop at the (2)_____?
M: No. It will stop at Union Street (3)_____. Get off the bus there and you will be able to see the (4)_____ one block down from there.

W: How will I recognize it?
M: It's a pink marble building with a (5)_____.
W: That sounds easy enough. Thank you for your help.
M: My pleasure. Have a nice day.

69

A. Listen & Choose   Choose the best answer.

1. How far should you drive on Greenville Avenue?
   (A) four blocks
   (B) four miles
   (C) four streets
   (D) four kilometers

2. When you're on Greenville, where should you turn right?
   (A) Main Street
   (B) Stop Light Street
   (C) University Drive
   (D) Wright Lane

Listen again. Fill in the blanks.

Take Highway 75 (1)_____ from Hampton Parkway. Take the Greenville Avenue exit off the highway. Drive for about four (2)_____. You will pass several stop lights while you are driving. At the stop light where Greenville meets (3)_____, turn right. This street will take you to the main entrance of the university.

B. Listen & Choose   Choose the best answer.

1. Which floor is the professor's office on?
   (A) first
   (B) second
   (C) third
   (D) fourth

2. What should you look for as you walk along the hallway?
   (A) a door
   (B) another hallway
   (C) a sign
   (D) office numbers

Listen again. Fill in the blanks.

Our professor's office is in Vesper Hall, but you shouldn't go in the building's main entrance. Instead, go in the doors on the (1)_____ of the building. Go up the stairs to the (2)_____ floor. Follow the hallway. It will turn left, but keep walking. When you see (3)_____ on the right, turn there and walk to the end of it. That's where Professor Smith's office is.

A. Picture Matching Listen to the dialog. Choose the correct picture.

 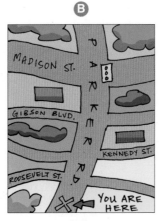 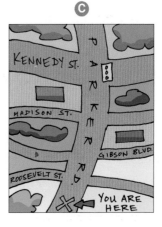

1.   (A)   (B)   (C)

2.   (A)   (B)   (C)

B. Listen & Choose Listen to the dialog and question. Choose the best answer.

1. (A) from a compass   (B) from the stars
   (C) from the sun   (D) from the south

2. (A) in another building   (B) near the front door
   (C) on the next floor   (D) outside the building

3. (A) a hotel   (B) a room
   (C) the pool   (D) the stairs

4. (A) in an airport   (B) in a hospital
   (C) in a school   (D) in a supermarket

5. (A) by the front door   (B) at the end of the aisle
   (C) on the bottom shelf   (D) under the cash register

6. (A) seats   (B) the box office
   (C) the exit   (D) the stage

7. (A) She is confused.   (B) She knows the way well.
   (C) She is hungry.   (D) She wants to go home.

Reading

A. Pre-reading Discussion

Talk about these questions.

1. Do you know which way is north right now?

2. Are you good at finding places and knowing directions?

3. If a man and a woman go on a driving trip, who usually drives? Why?

Many people believe that men are better in finding directions than women. Maybe that is why men usually drive when couples go somewhere. But is it really true that men are better at directions than women? Some researchers have tried to find out.

One man studying this question looked at men and women who were training to be soldiers. As part of their training, the men and women had to find their way through forests and over mountains. The researcher found an interesting difference between the men and women. Most of the men used the directions north, south, east, and west along with big things around them (like mountains or the sun) to find their way. On the other hand, the women found their way by going from one point to the next without imagining their larger environment. In this exercise, the men usually did better than the women.

Other researchers have studied how men's and women's brains work. Some say that men are better at solving puzzles and imagining objects. Women are better at using language and communicating.

B. Reading Comprehension

Answer the following questions from the reading.

1. Who did the researcher study?

2. Who did better at finding directions, men or women?

3. What do some researchers say women are better at than men?

Listening Test

Part I: Picture Description

Choose the statement that best describes what you see in the picture.

1.

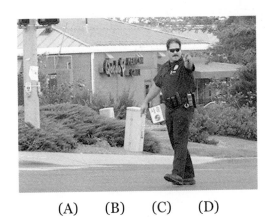

    (A)   (B)   (C)   (D)

2.

    (A)   (B)   (C)   (D)

3.

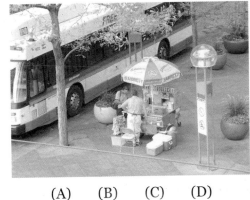

    (A)   (B)   (C)   (D)

4.

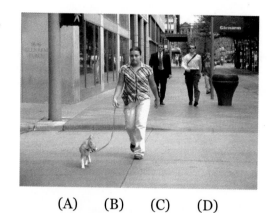

(A)   (B)   (C)   (D)

5.

(A)   (B)   (C)   (D)

Part II: Questions and Responses

Listen to the question and choose the best answer.

1. (A)   (B)   (C)

2. (A)   (B)   (C)

3. (A)   (B)   (C)

4. (A)   (B)   (C)

5. (A)   (B)   (C)

Part III: Short Conversations

Choose the best answer to each question.

1. Where are the speakers?
   (A) in a car
   (B) in a museum
   (C) in a restaurant
   (D) in a store

2. Where should the man go?
   (A) to another floor
   (B) to another part of the store
   (C) to another store
   (D) to another street

3. Which direction should the woman go?
   (A) east
   (B) north
   (C) northeast
   (D) The man does not know.

4. Where are these people?
   (A) in a bank
   (B) in a library
   (C) in a post office
   (D) in a theater

5. Which is true about the woman?
   (A) She does not like her dentist.
   (B) She has a dental appointment.
   (C) She is the man's dentist.
   (D) She works downtown.

Part IV: Short Talks

Choose the best answer to each question.

1. How should a person travel to this location?
   (A) by bus
   (B) by subway
   (C) by taxi
   (D) skiing

2. What do the instructions say NOT to do?
   (A) enter the mall
   (B) go up to the street
   (C) look for signs
   (D) take the green line

3. Where is the spa?
   (A) across the street
   (B) next to the main lobby
   (C) on top of the hotel
   (D) on the third floor

4. How can a person recognize the spa entrance?
   (A) It has glass doors.
   (B) The door is very small.
   (C) The hallway is long and wide.
   (D) There is a desk in front of it.

5. Where can a person get information on equipment in the spa?
   (A) at the hotel lobby's main desk
   (B) by calling a special number
   (C) at the spa's reception desk
   (D) from any hotel employee

A. Look & Listen   Listen to the dialogs.

B. Match   Listen again. Match the person with the situation.

1. Jason   · was sick
2. Billy   · is turning in homework
3. Jenny   · needs a pencil
4. Anne   · has to go home

C. Practice   Practice these sentences from the dialogs.

1. A: May I see your homework from last night?
   B: Yes, ma'am. Here it is.

2. A: I have to go home right after school.
   B: OK. I'll tell the other guys.

3. A: Can I borrow a pencil?
   B: Sure. Here you go.

4. A: I can explain last night's homework to you.
   B: That would be great. Thanks.

A. How would you answer? Listen. Write the answer.

> About twenty-five. Choir. Mr. Oliver.
> No, it wasn't. Yes. I think it's fun.

1. _____
2. _____
3. _____
4. _____
5. _____

B. How would you ask? Listen. Write the question or statement.

> What did you get on the exam? Do you like this class?
> What is your teacher's name? How long is the class?
> When is the test?

1. _____
2. _____
3. _____
4. _____
5. _____

C. Picture Description Describe the picture using the words below.

> graduate arm picture roses

_____

_____

_____

_____

Listen to the description of the picture.

A. Vocabulary   Listen to the words and repeat them.

1. (A) backpack   (B) notebook   (C) pen   (D) pencil
2. (A) essay   (B) exam   (C) homework   (D) test
3. (A) enroll   (B) fail   (C) graduate   (D) pass
4. (A) grade   (B) points   (C) score   (D) report card
5. (A) instructor (B) principal   (C) professor (D) teacher

Now listen to the dialogs and circle the word you hear.

B. Conversation Pictures   Listen to the dialogs and number the pictures.

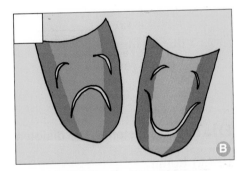

Now listen to the dialogs again and match the year in school with the activity.

1. freshman   · (A) acting
2. sophomore   · (B) sports
3. junior   · (C) studying
4. senior   · (D) writing

A. Dialog 1 Listen to the dialog and questions. Choose the best answer.

1. (A) He already ate lunch.   (B) He did not do the homework.
   (C) He is good at math.   (D) He wants to help the girl.

2. (A) He can't finish it quickly. (B) He does not like math.
   (C) He is a good student.   (D) He will get a good score.

Listen again. Fill in the blanks.

> W: Did you finish the math homework yet?
> M: No, I haven't even (1)_____ it.
> W: Too bad. I thought we could check our answers together.
> M: I was planning to do the homework (2)_____. Maybe
>   we can check it then.
> W: There is (3)_____ you can finish all those problems
>   during lunch.
> M: I can if you help me.

B. Dialog 2 Listen to the dialog and questions. Choose the best answer.

1. (A) home   (B) to see his teacher
   (C) to the nurse   (D) to the toilet

2. (A) He is lazy.   (B) He is lying.
   (C) He likes the nurse.   (D) He looks very ill.

Listen again. Fill in the blanks.

> M: Mrs. Wilson?
> W: Yes, Tom?
> M: I'm not feeling well. May I go to the (1)_____?
> W: What is the matter?
> M: I have a stomachache. I think it was (2)_____ I ate for
>   lunch.
> W: You don't (3)_____ at all, Tom. Maybe you had better
>   go see the school nurse.

A. Listen Choose the best answer.

1. Why did he think she is a high school student?
   (A) her age
   (B) her backpack
   (C) her books
   (D) her clothes

2. What year of high school is she in?
   (A) first
   (B) second
   (C) third
   (D) fourth

3. Which class is she probably taking?
   (A) biology
   (B) French
   (C) geometry
   (D) literature

B. Listen again Fill in the blanks.

M: Hi. My name is Tim.

W: Hi, Tim. I'm Martha.

M: I noticed your school (1)_____. What school do you go to?

W: I go to Longfellow High School. How about you?

M: I go to Central High. What (2)_____ are you in school?

W: I'm a (3)_____.

M: Me too! If we went to the same school, we would probably be in lots of the same classes.

W: Maybe. At Longfellow we get to choose classes to fit our interests, so I'm taking some extra (4)_____ classes. Do you like those kinds of subjects?

M: Uh, not really. I'm more into (5)_____ and English.

A. Listen & Choose   Choose the best answer.

1. Who might join this club?
(A) students who like art
(B) students who like math
(C) students who like sports
(D) students who like writing

2. What will the club make?
(A) a book
(B) a play
(C) a presentation
(D) a sport's competition

Listen again. Fill in the blanks.

I am glad to see that so many students at our school are interested in starting a (1)_____ club. Since this is our club's first meeting, we need to decide on how our meetings should be organized. I hope we can all share the (2)_____ that we write during this school year. One of our teachers, Mr. Greenwald, has volunteered to help our club put together a (3)_____ at the end of the year.

B. Listen & Choose   Choose the best answer.

1. Who is Ms. Stevens?
(A) a salesperson
(B) a secretary
(C) a student
(D) a teacher

2. What did Gloria do wrong?
(A) She did not go to class.
(B) She did not study at home.
(C) She did not take tests.
(D) She did not write an essay.

Listen again. Fill in the blanks.

Hello. This is Ms. Stevens. I'm a (1)_____ at Eastside Middle School. I wanted to talk with you about your daughter's poor (2)_____ this semester. Gloria has missed several (3)_____ already, and it is only the fifth week of school. I will try to call again tomorrow evening. I hope to talk to you then about this problem. Goodbye.

A. Picture Matching   Listen to the dialog. Choose the correct picture.

Ⓐ Ⓑ Ⓒ

1.   (A)   (B)   (C)

2.   (A)   (B)   (C)

B. Listen & Choose   Listen to the dialog and question. Choose the best answer.

1. (A) after school   (B) before lunch
   (C) during break time   (D) in class

2. (A) a classmate   (B) homework problems
   (C) studying together   (D) test results

3. (A) It is boring.   (B) It is difficult.
   (C) It is good.   (D) It is finished.

4. (A) He doesn't have time.   (B) He doesn't know.
   (C) He doesn't like sports.   (D) He doesn't play well.

5. (A) They are easy.   (B) They are getting worse.
   (C) They are improving.   (D) They are the same.

6. (A) go to a museum   (B) go to England
   (C) go to a theater   (D) go to the zoo

7. (A) read it   (B) saw it
   (C) took it   (D) wrote it

Reading

A. Pre-reading Discussion

Talk about these questions.

1. What time do schools end each day in your country?

2. Do many students spend time at school after classes finish? What do they do?

3. Who usually watches young children if both parents work?

Many high school students in the United States take part in school activities such as sports, choirs, bands, math clubs, science clubs, and theater activities. But after-school activities are not just for high school students. Many elementary schools also have after-school programs for students.

Most of the students in elementary after-school programs cannot go home when school ends because both parents work. These students are too young to stay at home alone. So the main purpose of these programs is just to watch the children until their parents can take them home. And the best part is that many of the programs in elementary schools are free for parents, unlike professional daycare centers that are usually very expensive.

The teachers in charge of the programs want the children to learn while they are there. So the programs may have a special time for children to do their homework. And many schools also keep the school library open for students. Students can go to the library to read books or to use the library's computers. But after-school programs are not "all work". There is also plenty of time for children to play on the school's playground.

B. Reading Comprehension

Answer the following questions from the reading.

1. Why do students usually go to after-school programs in elementary school?

2. How are some after-school programs better than day care programs?

3. What are three things children may do in an after-school program?

Listening Test

Part I: Picture Description

Choose the statement that best describes what you see in the picture.

1.

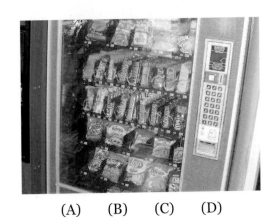

(A) (B) (C) (D)

2.

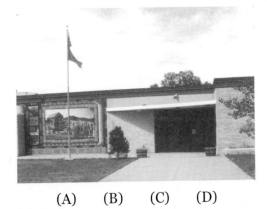

(A) (B) (C) (D)

3.

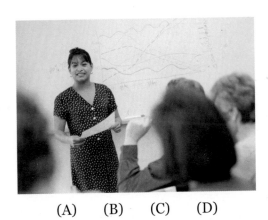

(A) (B) (C) (D)

4.

(A)　　(B)　　(C)　　(D)

5.

(A)　　(B)　　(C)　　(D)

Part II: Questions and Responses

Listen to the question and choose the best answer.

1. (A)　　(B)　　(C)

2. (A)　　(B)　　(C)

3. (A)　　(B)　　(C)

4. (A)　　(B)　　(C)

5. (A)　　(B)　　(C)

Part III: Short Conversations

Choose the best answer to each question.

1. What does the girl request?
   (A) a special time to study before the test
   (B) another day for the exam
   (C) extra points on her last test
   (D) one question from the exam to be changed

2. How did he think she acted in class?
   (A) confident
   (B) nervous
   (C) silly
   (D) worried

3. What is her response to his request?
   (A) I don't understand.
   (B) I'll think about it.
   (C) No way.
   (D) OK.

4. What does the woman say about the subject?
   (A) She finds it too difficult to continue.
   (B) She hopes the class will finish soon.
   (C) She'll need to know it in the future.
   (D) She won't use it in her career.

5. What will she probably buy?
   (A) a dictionary
   (B) a grammar book
   (C) a notebook
   (D) some coffee

Part IV: Short Talks

Choose the best answer to each question.

1. Where does this teacher probably work?
   (A) at an elementary school
   (B) at a high school
   (C) at a university
   (D) at a community college

2. What is the speaker's opinion of his career?
   (A) It is boring.
   (B) It is frustrating.
   (C) It is satisfying.
   (D) The pay is very good.

3. What does the student do before school starts?
   (A) exercises
   (B) practices driving
   (C) studies with friends
   (D) works in a donut store

4. When does the student study music?
   (A) in her first class
   (B) before lunch
   (C) right after lunch
   (D) after school

5. What does she like about her classes?
   (A) the books
   (B) the classmates
   (C) the homework
   (D) the teachers

Sports

A. Look & Listen Listen to the dialogs.

B. Match Listen again. Match the person with the action.

1. Sally · do a trick
2. Lisa · kick a ball
3. Matt · throw a ball
4. Joe · ride a skateboard

C. Practice Practice these sentences from the dialogs.

1. A: Here's my glove. Is it too big?
   B: No, I think it fits alright.

2. A: How can I kick the ball harder?
   B: Try using the top of your foot instead of the side.

3. A: I can do a cool trick with a Frisbee.
   B: What is it?

4. A: Have you been skateboarding long?
   B: Since I was about thirteen.

A. How would you answer? Listen. Write the answer.

> My friend.   No, there isn't.   On the school field.
> Twice a week.   Yes, I do.

1. _____
2. _____
3. _____
4. _____
5. _____

B. How would you ask? Listen. Write the question or statement.

> Have you played squash before?   Is water skiing fun?
> Where do you exercise?   How often do you play basketball?
> Who did you play with?

1. _____
2. _____
3. _____
4. _____
5. _____

C. Picture Description Describe the picture using the words below.

> hold   dirty   ground   tackle

_____
_____
_____
_____
_____
_____

Listen to the description of the picture.

A. Vocabulary Listen to the words and repeat them.

1. (A) athlete   (B) coach   (C) player   (D) team
2. (A) beat   (B) lost   (C) tied   (D) won
3. (A) fast   (B) slow   (C) strong   (D) weak
4. (A) ball   (B) field   (C) goal   (D) racquet
5. (A) every day   (B) occasionally (C) often   (D) sometimes

Now listen to the dialogs and circle the word you hear.

B. Conversation Pictures Listen to the dialogs and number the pictures.

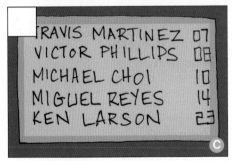

Now listen to the dialogs again and choose the correct topic of the conversation.

1. (A) a player   (B) food   (C) the coach   (D) the seats
2. (A) a player   (B) food   (C) the coach   (D) the seats
3. (A) a player   (B) food   (C) the coach   (D) the seats
4. (A) a player   (B) food   (C) the coach   (D) the seats

A. Dialog 1 Listen to the dialog and questions. Choose the best answer.

1. (A) daily   (B) at least once a month
   (C) every week   (D) a few times a year

2. (A) his team   (B) his equipment
   (C) his partner   (D) his skill

Listen again. Fill in the blanks.

W: How often do you play tennis?

M: Not as often as I'd like to play. I only play once or twice a (1)_____.

W: Have you been playing tennis for a long time?

M: Since I was (2)_____. I was actually on my school's tennis team.

W: You must be pretty good then.

M: I was better when I played regularly. Now I'm out of (3)_____.

B. Dialog 2 Listen to the dialog and questions. Choose the best answer.

1. (A) It is boring.   (B) It is in a building.
   (C) It is like pool.   (D) It is too hard.

2. (A) He is too old.   (B) He wants to exercise.
   (C) It is expensive.   (D) It is far away.

Listen again. Fill in the blanks.

M: Would you like to go bowling this afternoon?

W: No, it's too nice to spend the day inside a bowling alley. Let's do something (1)_____.

M: Like what?

W: I know! Let's go to the zoo.

M: The zoo is (2)_____. How about going swimming instead?

W: OK. That sounds (3)_____. Anything is better than bowling.

A. Listen   Choose the best answer.

1. According to the woman, how will exercise benefit him?
   (A) He will feel happier.
   (B) It will help him study better.
   (C) He won't get sick easily.
   (D) It will make him stronger.

2. What does the man think he needs in order to exercise?
   (A) a coach
   (B) a place to exercise
   (C) an exercise partner
   (D) exercise equipment

3. What does the man suggest they play?
   (A) a game
   (B) a team sport
   (C) a water sport
   (D) a two-player sport

B. Listen again   Fill in the blanks.

W: Do you exercise much?

M: Not really. I don't have time.

W: You should make time.
Exercise is good for your (1)_____.
You won't catch so many colds!

M: I know that, but I just can't force
myself to do it.

W: Try to find a sport or some kind
of exercise you enjoy, and then
it will be (2)_____ for
you.

M: I think the best thing is to find
a (3)_____ to exercise
with. Then working out won't
be so (4)_____.

W: I can work out with you.
Maybe we can play a sport
together. What do you like to
play?

M: I'm pretty good at (5)_____.
Do you like to play that?

A. Listen & Choose   Choose the best answer.

1. What sport is described by the speaker?
    (A) basketball
    (B) hockey
    (C) soccer
    (D) volleyball

2. Which is true about the final score of the game?
    (A) It was a very close game.
    (B) The other team had a lot more points.
    (C) Our team scored no points.
    (D) The other team scored fewer points.

Listen again. Fill in the blanks.

Our school's girl's (1)_____ team played their first
game last Friday. Unfortunately they lost the game. The
final score was (2)_____ to three. The other team's
offense and defense were both very strong. The best player
on our team was Nancy Taylor. She scored (3)_____.
Michelle Robertson scored our team's third goal.

B. Listen & Choose   Choose the best answer.

1. What does he think about the new players?
    (A) They are nervous.
    (B) They are proud.
    (C) They are strong.
    (D) They are young.

2. What do the new players need?
    (A) equipment
    (B) speed
    (C) techniques
    (D) understanding of the rules

Listen again. Fill in the blanks.

This year's team looks really good to me. When I went out
looking for new players, I really wanted to find kids who
were (1)_____ players. And I think I found them. All
the new boys on the team this year play (2)_____. Out
on the field, they really go for it. Some of them don't have
very good (3)_____ yet, but I can teach them that.
That's what I'm here for. That's why I'm the coach.

A. Picture Matching   Listen to the dialog. Choose the correct picture.

1. (A) (B) (C)
2. (A) (B) (C)

B. Listen & Choose   Listen to the dialog and question. Choose the best answer.

1. (A) hitting the ball   (B) how the playing area looks
   (C) scoring   (D) the equipment used

2. (A) asking for help   (B) coaching him
   (C) scheduling a game   (D) teaching him a rule

3. (A) none   (B) one
   (C) two   (D) three

4. (A) nothing   (B) two dollars
   (C) six dollars   (D) ten dollars

5. (A) counting the score   (B) looking for a place to play
   (C) starting a game   (D) taking a break

6. (A) bring water for her   (B) buy himself a drink
   (C) fix the machine   (D) take a shower

7. (A) zero to zero   (B) one to one
   (C) five to zero   (D) five to five

Reading

A. Pre-reading Discussion

Talk about these questions.

1. Which sports do you like to watch on television?

2. What sport or activity do you do most often?

3. How often do you do this sport or activity?

There is a difference between the most popular sport Americans watch and the most popular sport they play.

The most popular sports shown on television in the United States are football, basketball, and baseball. In other countries around the world, soccer is the most popular sport on television, but soccer is not usually shown on American television.

This is probably because it is not easy for television channels to show commercials during soccer games. In football, basketball, and baseball, there are many breaks during the game, and commercials can be shown in these breaks.

Although many Americans play football, basketball, and baseball in their free time, none of these sports rank as the most popular sport in America. The number of people playing this sport is much higher than the number playing these three sports. From a survey, sport researchers found that bowling was the most popular sport in the United States.

B. Reading Comprehension

Answer the following questions from the reading.

1. Which sports are popular on American television?

2. Why isn't soccer shown on American television?

3. What is the most popular sport in America?

Listening Test

Part I: Picture Description

Choose the statement that best describes what you see in the picture.

1.

(A)   (B)   (C)   (D)

2.

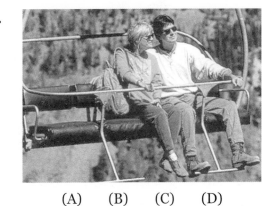

(A)   (B)   (C)   (D)

3.

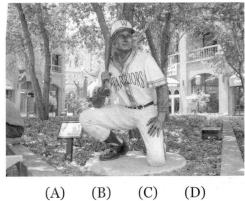

(A)   (B)   (C)   (D)

4.

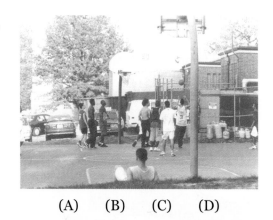

(A)　　(B)　　(C)　　(D)

5.

(A)　　(B)　　(C)　　(D)

Part II: Questions and Responses

Listen to the question and choose the best answer.

1. (A)　　(B)　　(C)

2. (A)　　(B)　　(C)

3. (A)　　(B)　　(C)

4. (A)　　(B)　　(C)

5. (A)　　(B)　　(C)

Part III: Short Conversations

Choose the best answer to each question.

1. What will the woman do?
   (A) give the man medicine
   (B) jog down the hill
   (C) play another game
   (D) stay home

2. What did Tim and Paula do at the party?
   (A) ate chips and salsa
   (B) broke the CD player
   (C) created a dancing mood
   (D) spilled ice on the floor

3. Which player does the man ask the woman to choose?
   (A) the best player in history
   (B) the player she likes most
   (C) the best player these days
   (D) the first player to come to mind

4. Why doesn't the man want to play?
   (A) It looks like a boring game.
   (B) The game is strange.
   (C) Only women are playing.
   (D) The teams are equal.

5. Which is probably true about Ben?
   (A) He is angry.
   (B) He is excited.
   (C) He is sick.
   (D) He is tired.

Part IV: Short Talks

Choose the best answer to each question.

1. What sport is described in this information?
   (A) baseball
   (B) rock climbing
   (C) tennis
   (D) wrestling

2. What part of the sport is described?
   (A) famous athletes from this sport
   (B) how to keep score
   (C) special actions before starting
   (D) how to play

3. How is salt used by the athletes?
   (A) to eat during rest periods
   (B) to make things dry
   (C) to purify things
   (D) to trick the other player

4. Who might benefit from this tip?
   (A) very young players
   (B) professional players
   (C) older players
   (D) female players

5. What does the tip explain?
   (A) choosing good equipment
   (B) keeping in shape
   (C) playing with a partner
   (D) strategies for scoring

Appearance

A. Look & Listen   Listen to the dialogs.

B. Match   Listen again. Match the person with the description.

1. the bride · dyed hair

2. a cousin · glasses

3. the groom · long hair

4. the father · mustache

C. Practice   Practice these sentences from the dialogs.

1. A: I didn't know you used to have long hair.
   B: Oh yeah. I had long hair for years and years.

2. A: Who is the boy wearing glasses?
   B: That is my cousin.

3. A: Do you think he looks different now?
   B: He looks a lot different now.

4. A: Your father looks much younger in this photo.
   B: All of his gray hair makes him look a lot older now.

A. How would you answer? Listen. Write the answer.

> Blue jeans and a T-shirt.   No, she doesn't.   Brown.
> Yes, he is.   He is a little taller than me.

1. _____
2. _____
3. _____
4. _____
5. _____

B. How would you ask? Listen. Write the question or statement.

> Does he have short hair?   How tall is she?
> How will I recognize him?   What color is his tie?
> What does she look like?

1. _____
2. _____
3. _____
4. _____
5. _____

C. Picture Description Describe the picture using the words below.

> twins   sandbox   wear   sit

_____
_____
_____
_____
_____

Listen to the description of the picture.

A. Vocabulary Listen to the words and repeat them.

1. (A) long   (B) short   (C) small   (D) thick
2. (A) body   (B) eyes   (C) face   (D) hair
3. (A) red   (B) brown   (C) blond   (D) black
4. (A) pants   (B) scarf   (C) shirt   (D) tie
5. (A) plump   (B) tall   (C) thin   (D) short

Now listen to the dialogs and circle the word you hear.

B. Conversation Pictures Listen to the dialogs and number the pictures.

A

B

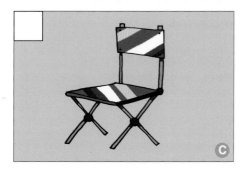

C

D

Now listen to the dialogs again and choose the number of 'yes' responses.

1. (A) none   (B) one   (C) two
2. (A) none   (B) one   (C) two
3. (A) none   (B) one   (C) two
4. (A) none   (B) one   (C) two

A. Dialog 1 Listen to the dialog and questions. Choose the best answer.

1. (A) her brother   (B) her father
   (C) her husband   (D) her uncle

2. (A) huge   (B) plump
   (C) skinny   (D) well-built

Listen again. Fill in the blanks.

> W: Excuse me. Have you seen an older man walking around? I'm
>   supposed to meet my (1)_____ here, but I haven't seen
>   him.
> M: What does he look like?
> W: He's got dark hair with a little gray in it. He's about 60 years old.
> M: Is he short and kind of (2)_____?
> W: Yes, he is. And he's got a (3)_____.
> M: I did see a man like that. He was sitting right over there about
>   ten minutes ago.

B. Dialog 2 Listen to the dialog and questions. Choose the best answer.

1. (A) It was expensive.   (B) It was too big.
   (C) It was too small.   (D) It was ugly.

2. (A) a bracelet on her wrist   (B) a chain around her neck
   (C) rings in her ears   (D) rings on her fingers

Listen again. Fill in the blanks.

> M: Who was that woman we met at the (1)_____ last
>   weekend?
> W: Which woman?
> M: The one with the long, curly red hair.
> W: You mean the red-head who was wearing the (2)_____
>   green dress and big gold (3)_____?
> M: Yeah, that was her! What was her name?
> W: That was my mother's friend, Dolores Maloney.

A. Listen   Choose the best answer.

1. Why does the woman call Kenneth?
   (A) He called her.
   (B) He found her wallet.
   (C) She has his wallet.
   (D) She is looking for something.

2. What does the woman NOT describe about the wallet?
   (A) its color
   (B) its material
   (C) its size
   (D) its texture

3. What will the man do?
   (A) buy her another wallet
   (B) call another location
   (C) mail her wallet to her
   (D) write down her name

B. Listen again   Fill in the blanks.

W: Lost and Found. This is Kenneth. May I help you?

W: Yes, I'm calling because I think I (1)_____ my wallet there this afternoon.

M: We've had a few wallets turned in. Can you (2)_____ the one you lost?

W: Yes, it is a black (3)_____ wallet.

M: Is your wallet smooth or does it have an alligator skin texture?

W: My wallet is smooth. And the clasp is (4)_____.

M: I'm sorry ma'am. No one has turned in a wallet like the one you've described.

W: Would it be possible to (5)_____ my name and number in case it does show up there?

M: Certainly, ma'am. What is your name?

Short Talks

A. Listen & Choose Choose the best answer.

1. What does the woman want to do?
   (A) buy furniture
   (B) paint furniture
   (C) repair furniture
   (D) sell furniture

2. Which is true about the chest-of-drawers?
   (A) It is antique.
   (B) It is almost like new.
   (C) It is damaged.
   (D) It is quite heavy.

Listen again. Fill in the blanks.

I can't come to the phone right now. Please leave a message after the beep. If you're calling about the chest-of-drawers that I'm (1)_____, you might want to know that it has five drawers and is painted (2)_____. The whole thing is in (3)_____ condition, so I'm asking for $50. Leave your name and number if you're interested. Thanks.

B. Listen & Choose Choose the best answer.

1. Who might need this information about snakes?
   (A) animal doctors
   (B) hikers in California
   (C) people with pet snakes
   (D) zoo keepers

2. Which body part of a rattlesnake is not described?
   (A) the eyes
   (B) the head
   (C) the tail
   (D) the teeth

Listen again. Fill in the blanks.

The only dangerous snakes in California are rattlesnakes. It is easy to identify rattlesnakes by the rattles on their (1)_____. Even baby rattlers have them. Rattlesnakes also have flat, triangle-shaped (2)_____. And if you are close enough to see a snake's eyes, look at its pupils. If the snake has (3)_____ pupils, it is not poisonous.

A. Picture Matching   Listen to the dialog. Choose the correct picture.

A    **B**    **C**

1.   (A)   (B)   (C)
2.   (A)   (B)   (C)

B. Listen & Choose   Listen to the dialog and question. Choose the best answer.

1. (A) a high school girl   (B) a teenage boy
   (C) a middle-aged woman   (D) an old man

2. (A) a coat   (B) a dress
   (C) a handbag   (D) a suitcase

3. (A) Carmen was short.   (B) Carmen was tall.
   (C) The woman was fat.   (D) The woman was thin.

4. (A) He lost it.   (B) He sold it.
   (C) It hurt him.   (D) It is famous.

5. (A) It was dead.   (B) It was his dog.
   (C) It was big.   (D) It was someone's pet.

6. (A) her eye color   (B) her hair color
   (C) her height   (D) her weight

7. (A) her age   (B) her job
   (C) her height   (D) her interests

Reading

A. Pre-reading Discussion

Talk about these questions.

1. What is your race?

2. What percent of the population in your country is this race?

3. Which races have the largest populations in England?

Imagine a person from England. Did you imagine a White person? If you did, that was a good picture of the average person from England. In fact, most of the population of England and Wales is White. If you visit England, nine out of ten people you see will be White.

Although the number of non-Whites in England has grown since World War II, there are only two places in England where minorities have become majorities. In Newham and Brent, two parts of London, races other than White make up more than 50% of the population in these areas.

According to the 2001 census of England, 91% of the population is White. This includes Whites from Ireland, Europe, Australia, New Zealand, the United States, and other countries. People from Asia make up the next largest population of people in England. Two out of every 100 people in England are from India. Three out of every 200 people are from Pakistan. And out of every 400 people two are from Bangladesh and two more are from China.

Blacks are a smaller minority than Asians in England. There are almost equal numbers of Blacks from Africa and the Caribbean. About two out of every 100 people are Black: one African and one Caribbean.

B. Reading Comprehension

Answer the following questions from the reading.

1. What percent of the British population is White?

2. How are Newham and Brent different than other places in England?

3. Which population is the largest minority in England?

Listening Test

Part I: Picture Description

Choose the statement that best describes what you see in the picture.

1.

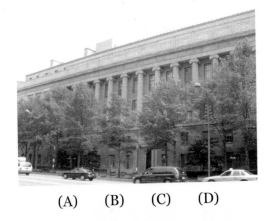

(A)   (B)   (C)   (D)

2.

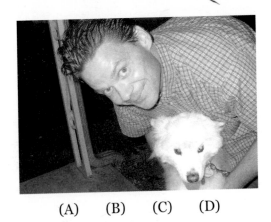

(A)   (B)   (C)   (D)

3.

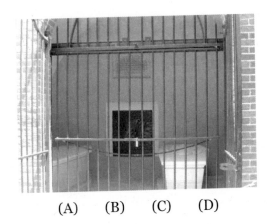

(A)   (B)   (C)   (D)

4.

(A)   (B)   (C)   (D)

5.

(A)   (B)   (C)   (D)

Part II: Questions and Responses

Listen to the question and choose the best answer.

1. (A)   (B)   (C)

2. (A)   (B)   (C)

3. (A)   (B)   (C)

4. (A)   (B)   (C)

5. (A)   (B)   (C)

Part III: Short Conversations

Choose the best answer to each question.

1. Where are these people?
   (A) at a restaurant
   (B) at the airport
   (C) in a clothing store
   (D) in a museum

2. What makes Jennifer look older?
   (A) her clothes
   (B) her haircut
   (C) her weight
   (D) her glasses

3. What does the woman think?
   (A) It is cheap.
   (B) It is large.
   (C) It is stolen.
   (D) It is ugly.

4. What difference did the man notice about the woman?
   (A) her clothes
   (B) her height
   (C) her looks
   (D) her jewelry

5. Why does the woman want her money back?
   (A) The item does not work.
   (B) The item is damaged.
   (C) The item is expensive.
   (D) The item is the wrong size.

Part IV: Short Talks

Choose the best answer to each question.

1. What is being advertised?
   (A) a book on child care
   (B) a health club
   (C) children's shoes
   (D) sporting equipment

2. Which is NOT a feature of this product?
   (A) It can change sizes.
   (B) It is made for children.
   (C) It is made of metal.
   (D) It works well in winter.

3. Who is the advertisement directed toward?
   (A) children
   (B) coaches
   (C) parents
   (D) teachers

4. Which activity could this advice be applied to?
   (A) looking for a date
   (B) going to parties
   (C) studying at school
   (D) taking a photograph

5. What is the main idea?
   (A) take your time
   (B) tell the truth
   (C) think before you speak
   (D) work hard

Weather

A. Look & Listen Listen to the dialogs.

B. Match Listen again. Match each item and the reason.

1. no jacket   · no tanning
2. hat   · shade
3. umbrella   · sunny
4. no swimming suit   · warm

C. Practice Practice these sentences from the dialogs.

1. A: Do you think I'll need a jacket?
   B: I don't think so. I heard we will have warm weather all weekend.

2. A: Are you taking a hat? It will be very sunny at the beach.
   B: That's a good idea.

3. A: Why are you taking your umbrella? It won't rain.
   B: I am going to carry it for shade.

4. A: Don't you want to go in the water when you get hot?
   B: No. I don't like to swim in the ocean.

A. How would you answer? Listen. Write the answer.

> No, I haven't.   I think so.   Not very cold.
> Yes, you will.   No, it didn't.

1. _____
2. _____
3. _____
4. _____
5. _____

B. How would you ask? Listen. Write the question or statement.

> Do you think it will rain?   How hot is it?   Will I need my umbrella?
> Didn't the weatherman say it would snow?
> Would you like to play tennis?

1. _____
2. _____
3. _____
4. _____
5. _____

C. Picture Description Describe the picture using the words below.

> cold   snow   build   mittens

_____
_____
_____
_____
_____

Listen to the description of the picture.

A. Vocabulary — Listen to the words and repeat them.

1. (A) breeze   (B) cloud   (C) rain   (D) snow

2. (A) cold   (B) cool   (C) hot   (D) warm

3. (A) coat   (B) jacket   (C) umbrella   (D) sunscreen

4. (A) humid   (B) icy   (C) sunny   (D) windy

5. (A) blizzard   (B) drought   (C) hurricane   (D) tornado

Now listen to the dialogs and circle the word you hear.

B. Conversation Pictures — Listen to the dialogs and number the pictures.

Now listen to the dialogs again and choose the correct location.

1. (A) Manaus   (B) Prudhoe Bay   (C) Oranjestad   (D) Tummu

2. (A) Manaus   (B) Prudhoe Bay   (C) Oranjestad   (D) Tummu

3. (A) Manaus   (B) Prudhoe Bay   (C) Oranjestad   (D) Tummu

4. (A) Manaus   (B) Prudhoe Bay   (C) Oranjestad   (D) Tummu

A. Dialog 1 Listen to the dialog and questions. Choose the best answer.

1. (A) a large hat   (B) a raincoat
(C) a summer dress   (D) a warm coat

2. (A) clear skies   (B) rain
(C) snow   (D) fog

Listen again. Fill in the blanks.

M: Did you finish packing for your business trip?

W: Not yet. I plan to finish packing tonight.

M: Make sure you take your heavy **(1)**_____. I heard they're expecting a lot of **(2)**_____ in Chicago this weekend.

W: I hope it's not too bad. I'm supposed to fly back on Sunday afternoon.

M: Maybe things will clear up by then. I think most of the **(3)**_____ is expected on Friday and Saturday.

B. Dialog 2 Listen to the dialog and questions. Choose the best answer.

1. (A) the same as always   (B) hot and humid
(C) higher than usual   (D) lower than usual

2. (A) a hat   (B) an umbrella
(C) sunglasses   (D) sunscreen

Listen again. Fill in the blanks.

W: What a beautiful day!

M: Yeah. I haven't seen a blue sky like this in a long time.

W: At least all that rain earlier this week kept the temperature **(1)**_____.

M: Well, it might be **(2)**_____ and sunny today, so that means it will be hot.

W: You're right. Here, put on this **(3)**_____ before we go out.

M: Go out? Where are we going?

W: You're going to mow the lawn, and I'm going to water the garden.

A. Listen Choose the best answer.

1. What does the woman imply about the storm?
 (A) It was bright.   (B) It was dark.
 (C) It was loud.   (D) It was quiet.

2. Which is not mentioned as part of the storm?
 (A) hail   (B) lightening
 (C) wind   (D) rain

3. What can be inferred about the storm?
 (A) It was predicted early.   (B) It was typical for the season.
 (C) It was the worst in history.   (D) It was unusual for this time of year.

B. Listen again Fill in the blanks.

W: That was quite a storm we had last night.

M: There was a big storm last night? I didn't know that.

W: What? You mean the (1)_____ didn't wake you up?

M: No, I didn't hear a thing. It's too bad I slept through the (2)_____. I actually enjoy thunderstorms.

W: You would have loved this one. It had everything. There was thunder, lightening, (3)_____, rain...

M: Do you know how much rain fell?

W: I'm not exactly sure, but it must have been (4)_____ centimeters.

M: I hope I'm awake the next time a big storm like that blows through.

W: I bet you'll get to see one soon. This is the (5)_____ for storms like that.

A. Listen & Choose   Choose the best answer.

1. What does this advice refer to?
    (A) having fun in the summer   (B) avoiding skin problems
    (C) growing plants   (D) working outside in hot weather

2. Which is true in this kind of weather?
    (A) People get tired faster.   (B) People have darker skin.
    (C) People sweat more.   (D) People work more.

Listen again. Fill in the blanks.

Now that it is August, we can expect hot and (1)_____ days for the next few weeks. I know a lot of people are going to be working in their yards and gardens, but it is important to remember to be careful. Do yard work in the morning or in the evening when the temperature is (2)_____. And drink lots of water because this humid weather will make you (3)_____ more than usual.

B. Listen & Choose   Choose the best answer.

1. Where are the resorts with more snow?
    (A) in the east   (B) in the north
    (C) in the south   (D) in the west

2. Which is true about resorts close to this area?
    (A) They don't have any snow.   (B) They have snow made by machines.
    (C) They have lots of snowmen.   (D) They will close for the weekend.

Listen again. Fill in the blanks.

Most of the ski resorts in our area should have (1)_____ conditions over the weekend. The mixed rain and snow earlier this week did not hurt much or help much the snow on the slopes. Some of the resorts further (2)_____ have reported 6-10 centimeters of new snow. But resorts in our area are still relying on (3)_____ snow to keep the runs open. Clear skies are predicted all weekend, so get out there and enjoy it!

A. Picture Matching Listen to the dialog. Choose the correct picture.

Ⓐ Ⓑ Ⓒ

1.	(A)	(B)	(C)
2.	(A)	(B)	(C)

B. Listen & Choose Listen to the dialog and question. Choose the best answer.

1. (A) It is cold outside. (B) It is raining.
   (C) The fog is lifting. (D) The wind is blowing.

2. (A) March is cold. (B) April is stormy.
   (C) May is warm. (D) Spring is terrible.

3. (A) cold (B) warm
   (C) much hotter (D) the same

4. (A) a big storm (B) heavy snow
   (C) light rain (D) mild breezes

5. (A) a blackout (B) a fire
   (C) a flood (D) a tornado

6. (A) cold and snowy (B) cool and windy
   (C) hot and rainy (D) warm and dry

7. (A) It was frightening. (B) It was great.
   (C) It was terrible. (D) It was unusual.

Reading

A. Pre-reading Discussion

Talk about these questions.

1. What is the best time of year to visit your country?
2. Does your country have a rainy season or a dry season? If yes, when?
3. What is the worst weather you have experienced in your hometown?

If you plan to travel to Hawaii, don't worry about the weather. It is always "the best season" to visit the islands.

During most of the year, there are breezes blowing across the Hawaiian Islands. These are called the ocean "trade" winds because they helped trading ships travel to and from the islands. Sometimes during the year, the usual trade winds stop and then the wind comes from the south. This is the most humid time of the year in Hawaii.

The rainy season for Hawaii begins in November and ends in April. But that

does not mean that is a bad time of year to visit. On most days, it usually only rains for a few hours, and then people can see beautiful rainbows.

The season for hurricanes around the Hawaiian Islands is from August through October. But in Honolulu, where most people live, the hurricanes are rarely severe. Most of the time, hurricanes only produce stronger than normal winds.

B. Reading Comprehension

Answer the following questions from the reading.

1. What weather condition produces high humidity for Hawaii?
2. What can you see in Hawaii if you visit during the rainy season?
3. According to the reading, should people in Honolulu worry about hurricanes?

Listening Test

Part I: Picture Description

Choose the statement that best describes what you see in the picture.

1.

(A)   (B)   (C)   (D)

2.

(A)   (B)   (C)   (D)

3.

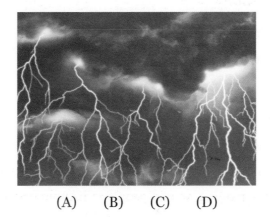

(A)   (B)   (C)   (D)

4.

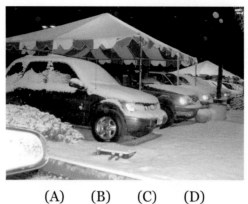

(A)   (B)   (C)   (D)

5.

(A)   (B)   (C)   (D)

Part II: Questions and Responses

Listen to the question and choose the best answer.

1. (A)   (B)   (C)

2. (A)   (B)   (C)

3. (A)   (B)   (C)

4. (A)   (B)   (C)

5. (A)   (B)   (C)

Part III: Short Conversations

Choose the best answer to each question.

1. What will the man do?
   (A) give her his umbrella
   (B) pick up her suitcase
   (C) take her in his car
   (D) wait for the rain to stop

2. What will he open?
   (A) the door
   (B) the window
   (C) the door and the window
   (D) the closet door

3. What kind of weather does the woman expect?
   (A) cold
   (B) hot
   (C) humid
   (D) dry

4. How does the man describe the sky?
   (A) clear
   (B) cloudy
   (C) gray
   (D) overcast

5. Which is true about the weather in this place in winter?
   (A) Hail often falls.
   (B) Ice never melts.
   (C) It is extremely wet.
   (D) It is very dry.

Part IV: Short Talks

Choose the best answer to each question.

1. Which is true about the weather on Tuesday and Wednesday?
   (A) It will rain and hail.
   (B) It will rain continuously.
   (C) It will rain off and on.
   (D) It won't rain at all.

2. What is the prediction for Saturday's weather?
   (A) cloudy skies
   (B) rain
   (C) strong winds
   (D) lots of sunshine

3. What does this advice refer to?
   (A) choosing clothing
   (B) predicting the weather
   (C) preparing for a storm
   (D) protecting your skin

4. Which item is NOT suggested for use?
   (A) a long-sleeved shirt
   (B) shorts
   (C) sunglasses
   (D) sun lotion

5. When should a person put on sun lotion?
   (A) before going outdoors
   (B) right after going outdoors
   (C) thirty minutes after going out
   (D) at two o'clock in the afternoon

Warm-up

A. Look & Listen Listen to the dialogs.

B. Match Listen again. Match the instruction with the action.

1. choose	· the number
2. remember	· the bar code
3. press	· the button
4. stick on	· the bananas

C. Practice Practice these sentences from the dialogs.

1. A: It's easy. I can show you how to use it.
   B: What do I do first?

2. A: What's next?
   B: You have to remember those numbers and punch them into the machine.

3. A: Do I punch in the number here on this keypad?
   B: Yes. Put in the number and press enter.

4. A: I guess I should put them in a bag before I weigh them.
   B: Right. See. It's easy to use the machine.

A. How would you answer? Listen. Write the answer.

No, I didn't.	First, turn it on.	Like this.
No, it's not.	Sure. What do you need?	

1. _____
2. _____
3. _____
4. _____
5. _____

B. How would you ask? Listen. Write the question or statement.

Are we finished?	Is this right?	Where are they?
Can we do this by ourselves?	Have you done this before?	

1. _____
2. _____
3. _____
4. _____
5. _____

C. Picture Description Describe the picture using the words below.

build	instructions	hammer	nails

_____

_____

_____

_____

_____

Listen to the description of the picture.

A. Vocabulary   Listen to the words and repeat them.

1. (A) first   (B) next   (C) then   (D) finally
2. (A) difficult   (B) easy   (C) hard   (D) simple
3. (A) directions   (B) instructions (C) rules   (D) steps
4. (A) how   (B) what   (C) when   (D) why
5. (A) after   (B) before   (C) until   (D) while

Now listen to the dialogs and circle the word you hear.

B. Conversation Pictures   Listen to the dialogs and number the pictures.

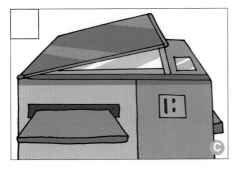
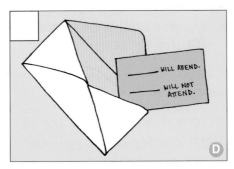

Now listen to the dialogs again and choose the correct length of time.

1. (A) now   (B) less than one minute   (C) many hours   (D) next week
2. (A) now   (B) less than one minute   (C) many hours   (D) next week
3. (A) now   (B) less than one minute   (C) many hours   (D) next week
4. (A) now   (B) less than one minute   (C) many hours   (D) next week

A. Dialog 1 Listen to the dialog and questions. Choose the best answer.

1. (A) Her card is not good.   (B) She can't read the machine.
   (C) The machine is broken.   (D) She lost all of her money.

2. (A) a PIN number   (B) cash
   (C) the amount she wants   (D) her card

Listen again. Fill in the blanks.

> W: Oh no! All of the words on this ATM machine's screen are in Chinese.
> M: I can help you. I know a little Chinese.
> W: I already put (1)_____ into the machine. What do I do now?
> M: If you want to take money out, press the (2)_____ button over here. Then put in the amount you want.
> W: Now what?
> M: Now it's asking for your (3)_____.
> W: Oh. It worked! Thanks a lot for your help.

B. Dialog 2 Listen to the dialog and questions. Choose the best answer.

1. (A) by playing all the cards   (B) by playing any card
   (C) by playing the bottom card   (D) by playing the top card

2. (A) play another two cards   (B) put in more money
   (C) stop the game   (D) take the cards back

Listen again. Fill in the blanks.

> W: Give me the cards and I'll teach you a fun card game.
> M: OK. How do you play?
> W: You take half the cards and I take the other half. Now we both put our (1)_____ cards down on the table.
> M: I have a seven and you have a nine.
> W: Since my card is higher, I (2)_____ of them. Now we put down another card.
> M: What if both of our cards are the same number?
> W: Then we put down (3)_____ and the higher player takes all four cards on the table.

A. Listen   Choose the best answer.

1. What are these instructions for?
    (A) buying flowers   (B) drying flowers
    (C) growing flowers   (D) naming flowers

2. What should the woman remove from the roses?
    (A) bugs   (B) flowers
    (C) leaves   (D) roots

3. How long will this process take?
    (A) several days   (B) a few weeks
    (C) more than a month   (D) She does not say.

B. Listen again   Fill in the blanks.

W1: That is a beautiful flower arrangement!

W2: Thanks. I (1)_____ the flowers myself.

W1: Really? Was it difficult?

W2: No. (2)_____ flowers is really easy. You can try it yourself.

W1: I have some roses at home I could dry. What do I need to do first?

W2: With roses, first take all of the (3)_____ and thorns off. Then cut the stems so they are about 30 or 40 centimeters long. Take six or seven roses and tie the stems together about 5 centimeters from the bottom. Then hang them (4)_____ so they can dry.

W1: How long does it take them to completely dry?

W2: I think two or three (5)_____ should be long enough.

A. Listen & Choose Choose the best answer.

1. What does this tip advise against?
   (A) hiking at night
   (B) leaving trash along the trail
   (C) walking too far
   (D) putting too much water into a container

2. When should a hiker do this?
   (A) several days before hiking
   (B) one day before hiking
   (C) the day of the hike
   (D) The tip does not say.

Listen again. Fill in the blanks.

When you go hiking this summer, carry a bottle of ice with you instead of a bottle of water. Take any small plastic bottle and fill it (1)_____ full of water. Don't completely (2)_____ the bottle, or it will break when it freezes. Put the bottle in the freezer (3)_____ before you go hiking. While you are hiking, the ice will melt, and you can enjoy a cool drink anytime during the day.

B. Listen & Choose Choose the best answer.

1. What does a person need in order to check his or her order?
   (A) an account name
   (B) a credit card number
   (C) a salesperson's name
   (D) an order number

2. Which service is offered through the company's website?
   (A) buying software
   (B) downloading software
   (C) previewing software
   (D) updating software

Listen again. Fill in the blanks.

Thank you for calling Software Central. Please (1)_____ the line and one of our customer service representatives will be with you shortly. If you are calling to check on an order you have already placed with Software Central, please have your (2)_____ ready. Customers may also (3)_____ software through the Software Central website at www.SoftwareCentral.com.

A. Picture Matching Listen to the dialog. Choose the correct picture.

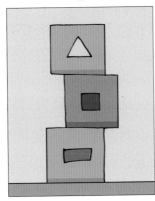
A

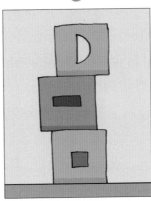
B

C

1.   (A)   (B)   (C)

2.   (A)   (B)   (C)

B. Listen & Choose Listen to the dialog and question. Choose the best answer.

1. (A) They will come back later.   (B) They will hear the number.
   (C) They will see the number.   (D) They will wait in line.

2. (A) BBQ Beef   (B) Chicken Soup
   (C) Grilled Steak   (D) Italian Chicken

3. (A) finding radio channels   (B) installing a program
   (C) playing a CD   (D) using a VCR

4. (A) check his passport   (B) find her lost passport
   (C) make a passport   (D) replace a passport

5. (A) a form   (B) her old passport
   (C) identification   (D) money

6. (A) tried a new kind of coffee   (B) drank too much coffee
   (C) fixed the coffee machine   (D) made bad coffee

7. (A) broke the machine   (B) did not wait long enough
   (C) put in too much coffee   (D) used bad water

R e a d i n g

A. Pre-reading Discussion

Talk about these questions.

1. Are you good or bad at remembering the names of new people?

2. Do you have any tricks for remembering names? If yes, what are they?

3. Can these tricks be used to remember other things?

Do you ever have trouble remembering people's names? If you do, here are some ideas you can try to help remember the names of people who you meet. The best way to remember someone's name is to repeat the name over and over. You can repeat the person's name while you talk to them. Or, if you have a moment or two while they are not talking to you, you can repeat their names in your mind. Repeating names in your mind is a good way to remember several names if you meet lots of new people at the same time.

Another trick you can use for remembering names is to connect the person's name to something else. If your friend Tom introduced you to Mike, you can remember them together as "Tom and Mike". Or you can connect the person's name to something about the person. If Sarah was wearing a silk sweater when you met her, it might help to remember her name as "Silk Sweater Sarah".

In case you forget someone's name, don't feel bad about asking them to tell it to you again. Everyone forgets names now and then. And after hearing it again, you'll probably remember it more easily next time.

B. Reading Comprehension

Answer the following questions from the reading.

1. What is the "best" way to remember someone's name?

2. What are two things names can be connected with?

3. What does the reading suggest if you forget someone's name?

Listening Test

Part I: Picture Description

Choose the statement that best describes what you see in the picture.

1.

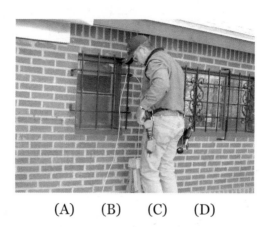

(A)   (B)   (C)   (D)

2.

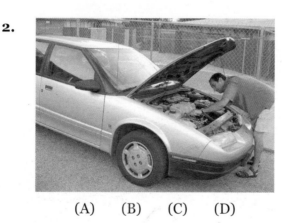

(A)   (B)   (C)   (D)

3.

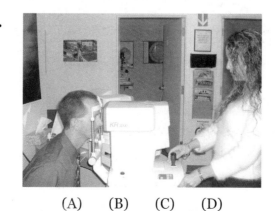

(A)   (B)   (C)   (D)

4.

(A)   (B)   (C)   (D)

5.

(A)   (B)   (C)   (D)

Part II: Questions and Responses

Listen to the question and choose the best answer.

1. (A)   (B)   (C)

2. (A)   (B)   (C)

3. (A)   (B)   (C)

4. (A)   (B)   (C)

5. (A)   (B)   (C)

Part III: Short Conversations

Choose the best answer to each question.

1. What is the woman probably using?
   (A) a bank machine
   (B) an office computer
   (C) a vending machine
   (D) a website

2. Where are they?
   (A) in a bicycle shop
   (B) in a hospital
   (C) in a post office
   (D) in a restaurant

3. Which is true about the fee?
   (A) He does not know about it.
   (B) Her friend will pay it later.
   (C) It's higher than before.
   (D) She can't use a credit card.

4. What does the woman tell the man to do?
   (A) hang the clothes on the line
   (B) put all the clothes together
   (C) separate the whites and colors
   (D) use warm water

5. What does the man suggest?
   (A) buying different chairs
   (B) coming back later to help her
   (C) deciding where to put the chairs now
   (D) inviting fewer people to the party

Part IV: Short Talks

Choose the best answer to each question.

1. What kind of advice is given?
   (A) how to act at parties
   (B) how to make friends
   (C) how to raise children
   (D) how to train pets

2. Which should you do when you feel angry?
   (A) ignore the problem
   (B) play a game
   (C) share your feelings
   (D) wait and calm down

3. When should you NOT choose to ignore bad behavior?
   (A) if a child could get hurt
   (B) if other people complain
   (C) if someone sees you
   (D) if you are embarrassed

4. Who might need to use this tip?
   (A) someone choosing a career
   (B) someone fixing a house
   (C) someone looking for an apartment
   (D) someone working in an office

5. What is the benefit of following this tip?
   (A) a safer home
   (B) better quality results
   (C) good friends
   (D) more money

Stories

A. Look & Listen Listen to the dialogs.

B. Match Listen again. Match the day and the event.

1. every day   · ate crayfish
2. last day   · had coffee in the French Quarter
3. Saturday   · heard a jazz band
4. first day   · walked by the Mississippi River

C. Practice Practice these sentences from the dialogs.

1. A: Are these the pictures from your trip?
   B: Uh-huh. This picture is of me and my friend.

2. A: You have heard that the city is famous for jazz, haven't you?
   B: No, I didn't know that.

3. A: Where was this picture taken?
   B: That was the day we went walking beside the river.

4. A: Did you like them?
   B: They're delicious! If you ever go there, you should try them.

A. How would you answer? Listen. Write the answer.

> He was nervous.   I fell into the water.   In Sydney.
> Me and two of my friends.   Two years ago.

1. _____
2. _____
3. _____
4. _____
5. _____

B. How would you ask? Listen. Write the question or statement.

> Can you tell us a joke?   Should I tell you how it ends?
> Were you hurt?   What did you do?   Where was it?

1. _____
2. _____
3. _____
4. _____
5. _____

C. Picture Description Describe the picture using the words below.

> night   tell   listen   campfire

_____

_____

_____

_____

_____

_____

Listen to the description of the picture.

A. Vocabulary Listen to the words and repeat them.

1. (A) experience   (B) trip   (C) vacation   (D) weekend
2. (A) excellent   (B) great   (C) terrific   (D) wonderful
3. (A) afterward   (B) in the end   (C) so   (D) meanwhile
4. (A) awful   (B) horrible   (C) lousy   (D) terrible
5. (A) all of a sudden (B) just then   (C) suddenly   (D) out of the blue

Now listen to the dialogs and circle the word you hear.

B. Conversation Pictures Listen to the dialogs and number the pictures.

Now listen to the dialogs again and choose who likes the movie described.

1. (A) woman   (B) man   (C) both
2. (A) woman   (B) man   (C) both
3. (A) woman   (B) man   (C) both
4. (A) woman   (B) man   (C) both

A. Dialog 1   Listen to the dialog and questions. Choose the best answer.

1. (A) his cat   (B) ice cream
     (C) milk   (D) the keys

2. (A) It got a flat tire.   (B) Its engine stopped.
     (C) It started moving.   (D) It was broken.

Listen again. Fill in the blanks.

M: Did I ever tell you about the time I locked (1)_____ in my car?

W: No. What happened?

M: I went to the store to buy some milk. I thought I'd only be in the store for a minute, so I didn't (2)_____ the engine.

W: Uh-oh. And then you locked the door when you got out of the car?

M: Yeah. I guess it is my habit whenever I get out of the car. So my car was running, but I was locked out of it! By the time the man showed up to open my car door, my car was (3)_____.

B. Dialog 2   Listen to the dialog and questions. Choose the best answer.

1. (A) answer the phone   (B) clean the house
     (C) cook for him   (D) speak to him

2. (A) find a new job   (B) live with her mother
     (C) not speak to her   (D) pay twice as much

Listen again. Fill in the blanks.

W: I heard a funny story on the radio today.

M: Really? What was it?

W: A man who has to talk on the phone all day at work pays his wife $100 per day if she doesn't (1)_____ him when he comes home at night.

M: Wow! That sounds like easy money for her.

W: It would be except she works on a computer all day. Sometimes she feels like she has to (2)_____ him at night. And the radio report said they are now thinking of having a baby.

M: I wonder if she can talk then.

W: No. Her husband wants to keep the same deal. But she says he has to (3)_____ after they have the baby.

A. Listen   Choose the best answer.

1. What are they talking about?
(A) a book she has read
(B) a class he took
(C) a movie he has seen
(D) a play they will watch

2. What is mysterious about Gatsby?
(A) his house
(B) his job
(C) his past life
(D) his wife

3. What was her opinion of the story?
(A) It was boring.
(B) It was pretty bad.
(C) It was terrible.
(D) It was good.

B. Listen again   Fill in the blanks.

W: What is that book you're carrying?

M: It's *The Great Gatsby* by Fitzgerald. I have to read it for one of my classes.

W: Oh, I (1)_____ last year.

M: Really? What is it about?

W: It's about a rich man with a mysterious (2)_____.
He is in love with another rich man's wife. Of course lots of problems develop from this situation.

M: So it's a (3)_____ novel?

W: Not really. It's about the different (4)_____ in society and how people can't really change who they are inside.

M: Is it any good? Do you think I'll like it?

W: I thought it was pretty (5)_____.

A. Listen & Choose Choose the best answer.

1. Who had always dreamed of going to Egypt?
  (A) her aunt   (B) her mother
  (C) her uncle   (D) the girl

2. Which transportation did she NOT use?
  (A) boat   (B) bus
  (C) camel   (D) taxi

Listen again. Fill in the blanks.

I had a great time over the summer vacation. I went to
Egypt with my aunt and uncle. My **(1)**_____ always
wanted to go there, and my parents thought it would be
a good experience for me. It was! We traveled by bus and
(2)_____ in the city, but I also rode a camel in the
desert. And I'll never **(3)**_____ seeing the Great
Pyramid and the Sphinx.

B. Listen & Choose Choose the best answer.

1. What was Henry's opinion of the date?
  (A) It was expensive.   (B) It was fun.
  (C) It went badly.   (D) It went well.

2. When did Jane wash the dishes?
  (A) after the movie   (B) before eating
  (C) while talking   (D) until Henry went home

Listen again. Fill in the blanks.

Sam said to Henry, "I heard you **(1)**_____ for Jane on
your first date. How was it?" Henry told his friend, "It
was **(2)**_____! Jane insisted on washing the dishes."
Sam asked, "What was wrong with that?" Henry said,
"She wanted to wash them before we **(3)**_____."

A. Picture Matching Listen to the dialog. Choose the correct picture.

Ⓐ Ⓑ Ⓒ

1. (A) (B) (C)
2. (A) (B) (C)

B. Listen & Choose Listen to the dialog and question. Choose the best answer.

1. (A) She is busy.   (B) She is scared.
    (C) She found a ticket.   (D) She might see it.

2. (A) him   (B) his friend
    (C) his friend's sister   (D) his parents

3. (A) a kind wolf   (B) a strong wind
    (C) animals on a farm   (D) pigs' houses

4. (A) at school   (B) at the park
    (C) in a store   (D) on the bus

5. (A) a dog   (B) an announcement
    (C) candy   (D) toys

6. (A) They liked the same girl.   (B) They lived together.
    (C) They were neighbors.   (D) They were on the same baseball team.

7. (A) movie posters   (B) paintings
    (C) postcards   (D) nothing

143

R e a d i n g

A. Pre-reading Discussion

Talk about these questions.

1. Have you ever met a famous movie star?

2. If you saw a famous person on the street, would you say anything to her/him?

3. Have you been embarrassed in a store? What happened?

I heard this story from a friend of mine. She said it really happened to a friend's mother's friend.

One day this lady went into an ice cream store. She ordered a strawberry ice cream cone for herself. While she was waiting for it, she noticed a man standing beside her. She looked over and saw that he was Harrison Ford! This lady had seen all of his movies and loved him, but she didn't want to act like some crazy fan in front of him. Instead, she pretended to act cool, as if he was just another guy in the ice cream store.

When the lady got out of the store, she realized she didn't have her ice cream cone. She went back in to get it and saw Mr. Ford standing at the counter and smiling. She smiled back and then told the clerk in the store, "I forgot my ice cream cone."

Mr. Ford said, "No, you didn't. You put it in your purse with your change."

B. Reading Comprehension

Answer the following questions from the reading.

1. Who did the woman see in the ice cream store?

2. Why was he smiling at the woman?

3. Where was her ice cream cone?

Listening Test

Part I: Picture Description

Choose the statement that best describes what you see in the picture.

1.

(A)   (B)   (C)   (D)

2.

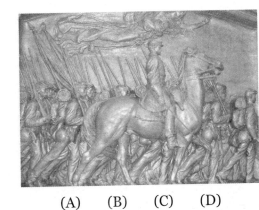

(A)   (B)   (C)   (D)

3.

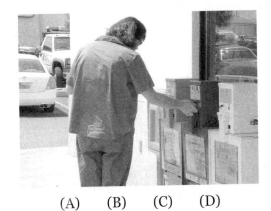

(A)   (B)   (C)   (D)

4.

(A)   (B)   (C)   (D)

5.

(A)   (B)   (C)   (D)

Part II: Questions and Responses

Listen to the question and choose the best answer.

1. (A)   (B)   (C)

2. (A)   (B)   (C)

3. (A)   (B)   (C)

4. (A)   (B)   (C)

5. (A)   (B)   (C)

Part III: Short Conversations

Choose the best answer to each question.

1. What does the woman think caused the problem?
   (A) an accident
   (B) holiday travelers
   (C) road construction
   (D) too many cars on the road

2. What did the woman do on her vacation?
   (A) saw famous places
   (B) spent time with her friend from Paris
   (C) took a photography class
   (D) took a cruise

3. What did their friend write about?
   (A) a bad place to live
   (B) his birthday party
   (C) looking for an apartment
   (D) the weather

4. What didn't she like?
   (A) the furniture
   (B) the price
   (C) the service
   (D) the view

5. What did the writer probably describe in the book?
   (A) her future
   (B) her hometown
   (C) her travels
   (D) her writing process

Part IV: Short Talks

Choose the best answer to each question.

1. What was difficult for him during his vacation?
   (A) paying high prices
   (B) the cold weather
   (C) speaking the language
   (D) walking everywhere

2. Which is true about the show he attended?
   (A) He didn't see it all.
   (B) He knew the story.
   (C) It was famous.
   (D) It was too long.

3. What kind of problem did the woman's husband have?
   (A) a cruel wife
   (B) a mental problem
   (C) a physical problem
   (D) fear of animals

4. How did the doctor help him?
   (A) gave him medicine
   (B) operated on him
   (C) talked to him
   (D) talked to his wife

5. Why does the woman ask the doctor to change her husband again?
   (A) So he can lay eggs.
   (B) So he will like chickens.
   (C) So he can fly.
   (D) So he can speak to chickens.

Editor

Eric Migliaccio

Managing Editor

Ina Massler Levin, M.A.

Illustrator

Vicki Frazier

Cover Artist

Barb Lorseyedi

Art Manager

Kevin Barnes

Art Director

CJae Froshay

Imaging

Rosa C. See

Publisher

Mary D. Smith, M.S. Ed.

S0-BTA-188

DECEMBER DAILY JOURNAL WRITING PROMPTS

GRADES K-2

DEC

DEC 19

DEC 25

SCHOOL OF EDUCATION
CURRICULUM LABORATORY
UM-DEARBORN Author

Maria Elvira Gallardo, M.A.

Teacher Created Resources, Inc.

6421 Industry Way

Westminster, CA 92683

www.teachercreated.com

ISBN-1-4206-3129-2

©2005 Teacher Created Resources, Inc.

Made in U.S.A.

CL
BY

ooo
C:l

Table of Contents

Introduction

More than ever, it is important for students to practice writing on a daily basis. Every classroom teacher knows that the key to getting students excited about writing is introducing interesting topics that are fun to write about. *December Daily Journal Writing Prompts* provides kindergarten through second grade teachers with an entire month of ready-to-use journal topics, including special holiday and seasonal topics for December. All journal topics are included in a calendar that can be easily reproduced for students. A student journal cover allows students to personalize their journal for the month.

Other useful pages that are fun include:

✣ **A Blank Calendar (pages 6 and 7)**

This can be used to meet your own classroom needs. You may want your students to come up with their own topics for the month, or it may come in handy for homework writing topics.

✣ **Word Banks (pages 40–43)**

These include commonly used vocabulary words for school, holiday, and seasonal topics. A blank word bank gives students a place to write other words they have learned throughout the month.

✣ **December Author Birthdays (page 44)**

Celebrate famous authors' birthdays or introduce an author who is new to your students. This page includes the authors' birthdays and titles of some of their most popular books.

✣ **December Historic Events (page 45)**

In the format of a time line, this page is a great reference tool for students. They will love seeing amazing events that happened in December.

✣ **December Discoveries & Inventions (page 46)**

Kindle students' curiosity about discoveries and inventions with this page. This is perfect to use for your science and social studies classes.

Motivate your students' writing by reproducing the pages in this book and making each student an individual journal. Use all the journal topics included, or pick and choose them as you please. See "Binding Ideas" on page 48 for ways to put it all together. Planning a month of writing will never be easier!

Monthly Calendar

DECE

1	2	3	4
The best part of December is…	The best birthday I ever had was…	If I were invisible, I would…	I get jealous when…
9	**10**	**11**	**12**
Before I go to bed, I…	For breakfast I like…	I want to talk to the principal about…	If I saw a U.F.O.…
17	**18**	**19**	**20**
Yesterday I…	A holiday tradition my family enjoys is…	Before the new year, I want to…	My favorite teacher is…
25	**26**	**27**	**28**
Santa Claus is…	If I had 14 brothers and sisters…	I couldn't stop laughing when…	If I could be anybody else, I would be…

Monthly Calendar *(cont.)*

M B E R

5	6	7	8
If I could fly	When I have trouble sleeping I usually…	My desk at school…	Now that it's winter…

13	14	15	16
The worst thing I ever did was…	I would love to meet…	If I could travel to the snow…	My favorite story is…

21	22	23	24
If I were my parents for a day…	Most people like Christmas because…	I have learned that Hanukkah is…	One day while playing with my friends…

29	30	31	Special Topic
Kwanzaa is…	One wish I have for the new year is…	A gift I really want is…	**Winter** Winter is a wonderful season because…

Blank Monthly Calendar

D E C E

1	2	3	4
9	10	11	12
17	18	19	20
25	26	27	28

Blank Monthly Calendar *(cont.)*

M B E R			
5	6	7	8
13	14	15	16
21	22	23	24
29	30	31	Free Choice Topic

The best part of December is _____

_____

_____

_____

_____

_____

_____

_____

_____

_____

The best birthday I ever had was _____

_____

_____

_____

_____

_____

_____

_____

If I were invisible, I would _____

_____

_____

_____

_____

_____

_____

_____

_____

_____

_____

I get jealous when _____

_____

_____

_____

_____

_____

_____

_____

_____

_____

If I could fly _____

_____

_____

_____

_____

_____

_____

_____

_____

_____

When I have trouble sleeping, I usually

_____

_____

_____

_____

_____

_____

_____

My desk at school _____

_____

_____

_____

_____

_____

_____

_____

_____

_____

_____

Now that it's winter _____

_____

_____

_____

_____

_____

_____

_____

_____

_____

Before I go to bed, I _____

_____

_____

_____

_____

_____

_____

                                    _____

                                    _____

                                    _____

For breakfast I like _____

_____

_____

_____

_____

_____

_____

_____

I want to talk to the principal about _____

_____

_____

_____

_____

_____

_____

_____

_____

_____

If I saw a U.F.O. _____

_____

_____

_____

_____

_____

_____

_____

_____

_____

_____

The worst thing I ever did was _____

_____

_____

_____

_____

_____

_____

_____

_____

_____

I would love to meet _____

_____

_____

_____

_____

_____

_____

_____

_____

If I could travel to the snow _____

_____

_____

_____

_____

_____

_____

_____

_____

_____

My favorite story is _____

_____

_____

_____

_____

_____

_____

_____

_____

_____

Yesterday I _____

_____

_____

_____

_____

_____

_____

_____

_____

_____

_____

A holiday tradition my family enjoys is

_____

_____

_____

_____

_____

_____

_____

Before the new year, I want to _____

_____

_____

_____

_____

_____

_____

_____

_____

My favorite teacher is _____

_____

_____

_____

_____

_____

_____

_____

_____

_____

If I were my parents for a day _____

_____

_____

_____

_____

_____

_____

_____

_____

_____

Most people like Christmas because

_____

_____

_____

_____

_____

_____

_____

I have learned that Hanukkah is _____

One day while playing with my friends

_____

_____

_____

_____

_____

_____

_____

_____

Santa Claus is _____

_____

_____

_____

_____

_____

_____

_____

_____

_____

If I had 14 brothers and sisters _____

_____

_____

_____

_____

_____

_____

_____

_____

_____

I couldn't stop laughing when _____

_____

_____

_____

_____

_____

_____

_____

_____

_____

If I could be anybody else, I would be

_____

_____

_____

_____

_____

_____

_____

_____

_____

_____

Kwanzaa is _____

_____

_____

_____

_____

_____

_____

_____

_____

_____

_____

One wish I have for the new year is

_____

_____

_____

_____

_____

_____

_____

New Year's Wishes

A gift I really want is _____

_____

_____

_____

_____

_____

_____

_____

_____

Winter is a wonderful season because

_____

_____

_____

_____

_____

_____

_____

_____

School Word Bank

alphabet	desks	map	recess
art	eraser	markers	report card
assembly	flag	math	rules
award	folder	note	science
binder	glue	office	scissors
board	grades	paper	spelling
books	history	pencils	study
bus	homework	pens	subject
children	journal	playground	teacher
clock	lessons	principal	test
crayons	lunch	reading	write

Holiday Word Bank

— December Holidays —		
Christmas	Hanukkah	Kwanzaa

African American	dreidel	Jewish
angel	drum	latkes
bells	elf	menorah
candy cane	eve	merry
candles	faith	ornaments
carols	family	presents
celebration	gelt	reindeer
chimney	gifts	Santa Claus
culture	gingerbread	stocking
dancing	Hebrew	tree
decorations	holly	wreath

Seasonal Word Bank

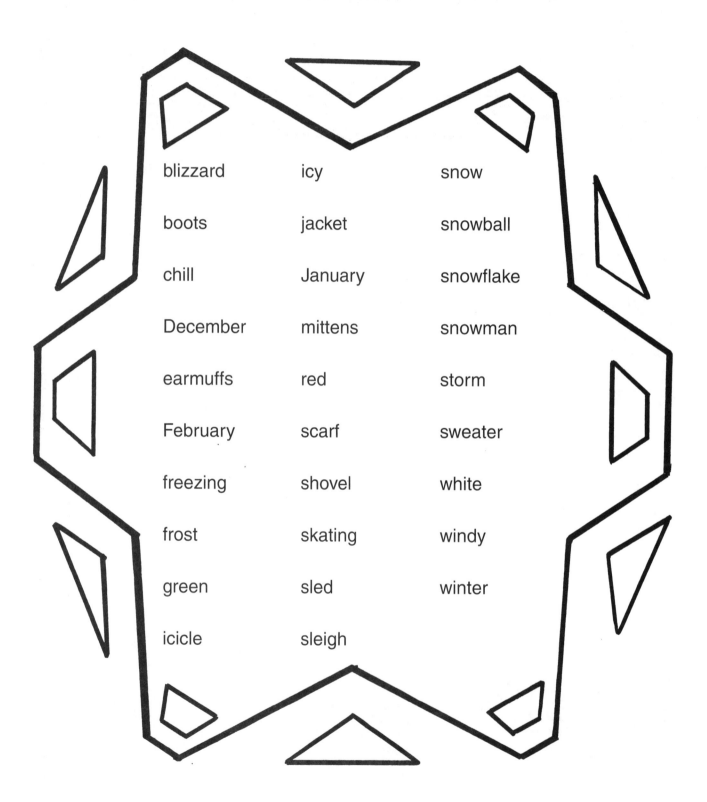

blizzard	icy	snow
boots	jacket	snowball
chill	January	snowflake
December	mittens	snowman
earmuffs	red	storm
February	scarf	sweater
freezing	shovel	white
frost	skating	windy
green	sled	winter
icicle	sleigh	

My Word Bank

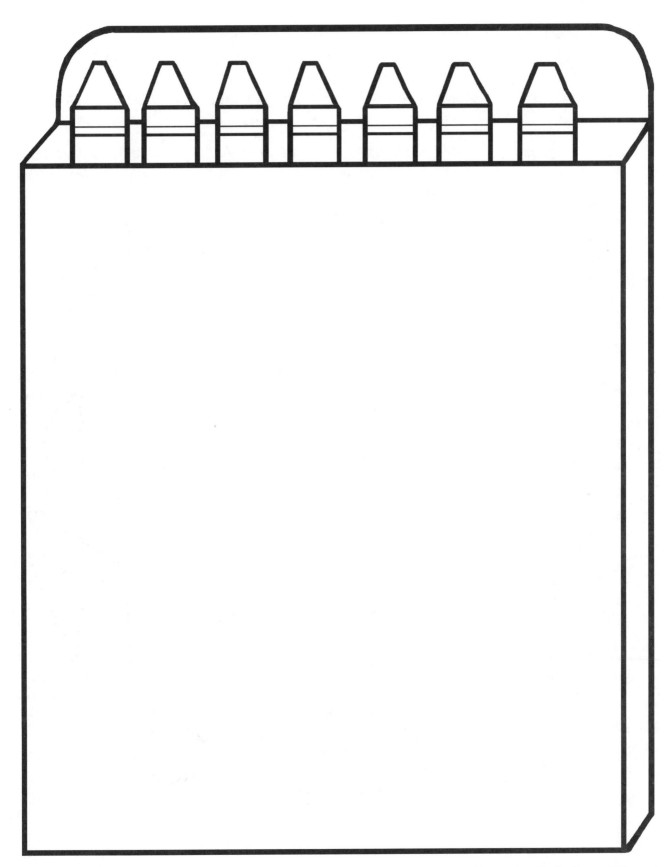

December Author Birthdays

1

Jan Brett
(b. 1949)

Hedgie's Surprise
(GP Putnam's Sons, 2000)
The Umbrella
(GP Putnam's sons, 2004)

2

Margriet Ruurs
(b. 1952)

Pacific Alphabet
(Whitecap, 2001)
Wild Babies
(Tundra, 2003)

2

William Wegman
(b. 1943)

Farm Days
(Hyperion, 1997)
Surprise Party
(Hyperion, 2000)

10

Douglas Wood
(b. 1951)

Rabbit and the Moon
(Simon & Schuster, 1998)
*What Teacher's
Can't Do*
(Simon & Schuster, 2002)

10)

Mercer Mayer
(b. 1943)

Just a Mess
(Golden Books, 1988)
All By Myself
(Golden Books, 2001)

14

Lorna Balian
(b. 1929)

Humbug Rabbit
(Humbug Books, 1997)
*Wilbur's Space
Machine*
(Holiday House, 1990)

16

E.B. Lewis
(b. 1956)

Talkin' About Bessie
(Orchard Books, 2002)
I Love My Hair!
(Megan Tingley, 1998)

21

Michael Berenstain
(b. 1951)

The Troll Book
(Bookthrift Co., 1982)
Baby Dinosaurs
(GT Publishing, 1997)

22

Jerry Pinkney
(b. 1939)

The Patchwork Quilt
(Dial Books, 1985)
Sam and the Tigers
(Dial Books, 1996)

24

Debra Barracca
(b. 1953)

Maxi, the Star
(Penguin USA, 1993)
A Taxi Dog Christmas
(Dial Books, 1994)

29

**Tracey Campbell
Pearson**
(b. 1956)
*Grandpa Putter and
Granny Hoe*
(Farrar, Straus &
Grioux, 1992)
Myrtle
(Farrar, Straus &
Grioux, 2004)

30

Rudyard Kipling
(1865–1936)

The Jungle Book
(HarperCollins, 1995)
Just So Stories
(HarperCollins, 1996)

December   Historic   Events

December 1, 1955
Rosa Parks, a black woman, refused to give up her bus seat to a white man in Montgomery, Alabama.

December 2, 1982
Barney C. Clark became the first recipient of a permanent artificial heart.

December 4, 1786
Franciscan Mission to the Indians was founded at Santa Barbara, California.

December 15, 1791
The first 10 amendments to the U.S. Constitution—known as the Bill of Rights—became effective.

December 16, 1773
On this date the Boston Tea Party took place. Nearly 350 chests of tea were dumped into the harbor by British patriots.

December 19, 1958
The U.S. Earth satellite Atlas transmitted the first radio voice broadcast from space—a Christmas greeting from President Eisenhower

December 21, 1913
The Pilgrims landed in Plymouth, Massachusetts.

December 22, 1956
At a zoo in Columbus, Ohio, "Colo" became the first gorilla born in captivity.

December 28, 1945
The U.S. Congress officially recognized the Pledge of Allegiance and urged its frequent recitation in America's schools.

December Discoveries and Inventions

1   **Basketball was created** by James Naismith in 1891 in Springfield, Massachusetts. He wanted to create a sport that could be played indoors during the winter months.

4   **The "shift" key was added to the typewriter** in 1878 by Remington & Sons. They unveiled the Remington 2, the first typewriter to come with the "shift" key, which allows users to switch between capital and lowercase letters.

7   **The phonograph,** invented by Thomas Edison, was first demonstrated in 1877.

9   **The first Christmas cards** were created in England in 1842.

14   **The South Pole was discovered** in 1911 by Roald Amundsen. He was joined by four companions and 52 sled dogs.

17   **Aztec Calendar Stone was discovered** in 1790. One of the wonders of the Western Hemisphere, the Aztec Calendar was found beneath the ground by workmen repairing Mexico City's Central Plaza.

       Wright Brothers made first powered flight in 1903 at Kitty Hawk, North Carolina. Wilbur and Orville Wright achieved the first successful flights in a gasoline-powered flying machine.

21   **First crossword puzzle was compiled** by Arthur Wynn in 1913. It was published in a supplement to the *New York World.*

23   **The transistor was invented** in 1947 by John Bardeen, Walter Brattain, and William Shockley of Bell Laboratories. The invention of the transistor led to a revolution in communications and electronics.

26   **Radium was discovered** in 1898 by French scientists Pierre and Marie Curie. They later won the Nobel Prize for Physics for discovering the element.

December
Journal

by

Binding Ideas

Students will be so delighted when they see a month of their writing come together with one of the following binding ideas. You may choose to bind their journals at the beginning or end of the month, once they have already filled all of the journal topic pages. When ready to bind students' journals, have them color in their journal cover on page 47. It may be a good idea to reproduce the journal covers on hard stock paper in order to better protect the pages in the journal. Use the same hard stock paper for the back cover.

Simple Book Binding

1. Put all pages in order and staple together along the left margin.

2. Cut book-binding tape to the exact length of the book.

3. Run the center line of tape along the left side of the book and fold to cover the front left margin and the back right margin. Your book is complete!

Yarn-Sewn Binding

1. Put all pages in order and hole-punch the left margin.

2. Stitch the pages together with thick yarn or ribbon.